The Holocaust: Events, Motives and Legacy

Martyn Housden

History Insights. Humanities-Ebooks, 2007

© Martyn Housden, 2007, 2008

The Author has asserted his right to be identified as the author of this Work in accordance with the Copyright, Designs and Patents Act 1988.

First published in 2007 by Humanities-Ebooks.co.uk.,
Tirril Hall, Tirril, Penrith CA10 2JE.

ISBN 978-1-84760-048-6 Ebook
ISBN 978-1-84760-066-0 Paperback

Contents

About the author — 5

Chapter 1 Anti-Semitism and Jewish policy up to 1939

1.1 Introduction — 6
1.2 Anti-Semites and what they said — 7
1.3 Hitler and Nazism — 10
1.4 From 1933 to 1939 — 13
1.5 Conclusion — 16

Chapter 2 The Pursuit of the Holocaust

2.1 Introduction — 17
2.2 1939–1940: Feeling the way — 18
2.3 1941. A new mood — 23
2.4 Garden of Eden — 26
2.5 The technology of mass murder — 28
2.6 Wannsee and beyond. — 29
2.7 Conclusion — 32

Chapter 3 The motives of the perpetrators

3.1 Introduction — 35
3.2 *Hitler's Willing Executioners*. Daniel Goldhagen — 37
3.3 *Ordinary Men*. Christopher Browning — 40
3.4 Bureaucracy and genocide — 42
3.5 Bureaucracy and the modern world — 44
3.3 Criticisms of bureaucratic theory — 45
3.4 Conclusion — 47

Chapter 4 How bystanders reacted

4.1 Introduction — 48
4.2 Germans as bystanders — 48

4.3	Other states: collaboration	51
4.3	Other states: resistance	54
4.4	The Vatican and the Holocaust	55
4.5	Allied statesmen	58
4.6	Conclusion	61

Chapter 5 The victims' view of the world

5.1	Introduction	62
5.2	Germany's Jewish citizens	64
5.3	Life in the ghettos	66
5.4	Leadership and choice	69
5.5	Making opportunities to escape and resist	71
5.6	Death camps and attempts to survive them	72
5.7	Jews as partisans	73
5.8	Conclusion	74

Conclusion: the legacy of the Holocaust

6.1	The Holocaust as 'moral resource'	75
6.2	Legal legacy. Nuremberg, crimes against humanity and international justice	77
6.3	Legal legacy. National responses	79
6.4	Political legacy. Uses and abuses of history	80
6.5	Conclusion. The root of it all—personal legacies	84

Selected bibliography   **88**

About the author

Martyn Housden is Reader in Modern History at the University of Bradford. His books include *Hans Frank. Lebensraum and the Holocaust* (Palgrave, 2003), *Hitler. Study of a Revolutionary?* (Routledge, 2000) and *Resistance and Conformity in the Third Reich* (Routledge, 1997). He has written and lectured widely for student audiences.

Chapter 1 Anti-Semitism and Jewish policy up to 1939

1.1 Introduction

Not only have Germany's borders changed extensively throughout history, but much of the territory inhabited by Germans has been shared with different national groups. In the north, Germans lived side by side with Danes; in the west they co-existed with Frenchmen; and in the east they shared land with Poles and Lithuanians. Across German territory, however, a rather different kind of population diversity took on world historical significance in the first half of the twentieth century. From Hamburg to Munich, from Cologne to Königsberg (today Kaliningrad), Christians lived side by side with Jews. At least this was the case until Adolf Hitler's National Socialist movement tried to eradicate Jewish feet from the soil on which Germans trod.

When Hitler came to power, less than one percent of the German population was Jewish. Their small numbers belied a long heritage because some Jewish communities had existed in the Rhineland when it belonged to the Roman Empire. Jewish families provided Germany with a number of notable individuals, not least the Hamburg-born composer Felix Mendelssohn (1809–1847). By and large, German Jews were well educated, respectable citizens who worked in professions such as banking, medicine and the law. Although long the subjects of prejudice, their position had improved across much of the nineteenth century, so much so that the years 1812 to 1871 have been called the 'decades of emancipation.'[1] The revolutions of 1848 saw Jewish liberation proclaimed and five Jews sat in the Frankfurt Parliament. Thereafter Prussia passed emancipatory laws on 3 July 1869. Later German Jews were accorded equal legal rights by the constitutions of the German Empire and the Weimar Republic.[2]

Unfortunately German history did not follow a single line of development and these progressive trends were counter-balanced by something darker. Even during the

---

1   H. Graml, *Antisemitism in the Third Reich* (Oxford: Blackwell, 1992), p. 39.
2   P. Longerich (ed.), *Die Ermorderung der Europäischen Juden* (Munich: Piper, 1989), pp. 11–2 and P. Pulzer, *The Rise of Political Anti-Semitism in Germany and Austria* (London: John Wiley, 1964), pp. 7–9. See also P. Pulzer, *Jews and the German State* (Oxford: Blackwell, 1992). Especially pp. 85–96 and pp. 271–86.

'decades of emancipation,' popular anti-Jewish feelings made it virtually impossible for Jews to find appointments in traditionally élite institutions like the Prussian civil service or officer corps. During the Weimar period, Jewish involvement in national and regional government remained limited for the same reason.[1] In other words, there was always a gap between what liberalising legislation said and how at least some people thought and acted. Anti-Semitism in Germany, as in other parts of Europe, had a long history and could run deep.

Talking in general terms, since some pagans hated Jews we can say that anti-Semitism seems to have pre-dated Christianity.[2] The Christian heritage, however, led to Jews becoming stigmatised in a unique way. Not just different, they were 'Christ-killers.' This characteristic, coupled with small numbers relative to general populations and a tendency to live in easily identifiable areas of towns, helped turn Jews into ideal scapegoats for any problems that might occur in wider society. This was particularly the case given that they often were involved in financial business (e.g. lending money) and so could easily be blamed for causing economic hardship. Their vulnerability was only increased by the lack of any Jewish 'home' state providing protection or refuge in the event of crisis. Consequently, over the centuries pogroms claimed the lives of hundreds of thousands of innocent Jewish men, women and children across Europe. For instance, in 1096 self-styled 'crusaders' massacred 50,000 in the Rhineland. Between 1648 and 1656, 25,000 were killed during uprisings in Ukraine. The Hep-Hep riots in Germany lasted from 1815 to 1830 and claimed another 30,000 Jewish lives. In Russia, 50,000 died during pogroms organised in the 1880s. The list of anti-Semitic outrages in European history goes on and on.[3]

1.2 Anti-Semites and what they said

It is worth observing that although anti-Semitic pogroms occurred at the end of the First World War, they did not happen in Germany. Jewish agencies counted 55 pogroms between December 1918 and mid-February 1919 in Ukraine which claimed 200,000 lives.[4] In this light, we can understand why during the post-war period a large number of Jews left the former Russian Empire for Germany. By comparison, it seemed the safer option. Nonetheless, a German strand of anti-Semitism really is

---

1 Pulzer, *Jews and the German State*, pp. 276–81.
2 R. S. Wistrich, *Anti-Semitism. The Longest Hatred* (London: Methuen, 1992), p. xviii.
3 S. S. Friedman, *A History of the Holocaust* (London: Valentine Mitchell, 2004), chapter 1.
4 Ibid, pp. 22–3; also A. Reid, *Borderland* (London: Orion, 1997), pp. 98–9.

impossible to ignore.

Martin Luther (1483–1546) was the originator of the Protestant Church. As a young man he recommended that Jews be treated well in the hope that toleration would encourage them to convert to Christianity. When this did not happen, Luther became so frustrated that three years before his death he wrote an outrageous manifesto. He said synagogues should be set on fire, Jewish homes and religious texts should be destroyed, and rabbis should be prevented from preaching on pain of death. His spleen seemed to know no bounds as he recommended that Jews be banned from travelling and lending money, indeed that all their possessions be confiscated. He wanted young, healthy Jews to be put to work for the benefit of the wider community and wondered openly if more able Jews should have their tongues cut out. In the end, however, he thought the only way to deal with Jews might be to expel them all.[1] These might have been the ideas of a member of Germany's intellectual élite, but they resonated among the popular classes. Hence the folklore collected by Jakob and Wilhelm Grimm (1785–1863 and 1786–1859) included tales such as 'The Jew in the Brambles' in which a dishonest Jew was executed for taking advantage of a servant.[2]

It is particularly easy to trace anti-Semitism among notable nineteenth century Germans. Richard Wagner (1813–83) was Adolf Hitler's favourite composer. In *Das Judentum in der Musik* he maintained that Jews had nothing original to contribute to the Arts. Wagner's operas also contained evil, scheming characters who fitted supposed Jewish stereotypes. Heinrich Treitschke (1834–96), a famous professor of History at Berlin University, made occasional anti-Semitic remarks, as did Karl Marx (1818–83)—notwithstanding the fact that his family had converted from Judaism.

It was, however, specifically in the latter part of the nineteenth century that anti-Semitism took on increasingly threatening characteristics. Partly this involved the re-discovery of old anti-Semitic insults and slanders. Hence, in 1871 Canon August Rohling re-discovered and publicised the accusation that Jews practiced the ritual murder of Christian children.[3] But anti-Semitism moved with the times too. Just as science was playing a greater role in society, so anti-Semites began to use an increasingly biological vocabulary. Consequently Jews were turned into contagious sources of infection. Biblical scholar and philologist Paul de Lagarde (1827–91) termed them

---

1   Friedman, *History of the Holocaust*, p. 9; A. S. Lindemann, *Anti-Semitism before the Holocaust* (Harlow: Longman, 2000), pp. 107–8.
2   Friedman, *History of the Holocaust*, p. 1.
3   D. Cohn-Sherbok, *Understanding the Holocaust* (London: Continuum, 1999), p. 21.

'trichnae and bacilli' who should be 'exterminated as quickly and thoroughly as possible.'[1] Others were inspired by discoveries about genetics or tried to apply in vulgar ways Charles Darwin's ideas about natural selection. So Arthur de Gobineau (1816–82) blamed the collapse of civilizations such as Rome and Greece on racial mixing. Hermann Ahlwardt (1846–1914) told the Reichstag that Jews were 'beasts of prey' who should be exterminated.[2]

This rise of biological anti-Semitism mattered because it closed the ultimate escape route from persecution which had always been open to Jews, namely baptism. So long as religious belief was the key characteristic associated with hatred, people could avoid it by converting. But as bigots began to 'biologise their thinking'—like the originator of the word 'anti-Semitism,' Wilhelm Marr (1819–1914), they thought more about 'blood' than religion—this possibility disappeared.[3] Biological thinking began to imply there was something intrinsically so 'wrong' about Jews that they could only be dealt with through complete segregation or annihilation.

The late nineteenth century also saw economic depression in Germany. In 1873 the Berlin stock market crashed and from then on anti-Semitism became an increasingly public matter. Adolf Stoecker (1835–1909) was court chaplain to the Kaiser and founded the Christian Social Party in 1878. It responded to electoral failure that year by adopting an anti-Semitic platform which targeted average German workers. It attracted enough support to win Stoecker a seat in the Reichstag which he kept until 1908. Popular support for anti-Semitic politics peaked in the 1890s. In 1893 the likes of the German Reform Party won a quarter of a million votes and 16 Reichstag seats. Even though electoral support declined from this point on, anti-Semitic parties still had 7 Reichstag deputies in 1907. In addition, pressure groups such as the Pan-German League (led by Heinrich Class after 1908) helped keep anti-Semitism alive.

Of course this was a period when other European states were also compromised by anti-Semitism. French anarchist Pierre Proudhon (1809–65) believed the Jewish race had to be 'sent back to Asia or exterminated.'[4] An Englishman, H.S.Chamberlain (1855–1927), wrote the Kaiser's favourite anti–Semitic work, *The Foundations of the Nineteenth Century* which was published in 1899. Also Austrian politicians such as Vienna's mayor, Karl Lueger (1844–1910), and the pan-German Georg von Schönerer both used anti-Semitism from time to time. The young Adolf Hitler, who lived in

---

1   Lindemann, *Anti-Semitism before the Holocaust*, p. 69.
2   P. W. Massing, *Rehearsal for Destruction. A Study of Political Anti-Semitism in Imperial Germany* (New York: Harper Brothers, 1949), pp. 300–1.
3   Pulzer, *Rise of Political Anti-Semitism*, pp. 49–50.
4   Cohn-Sherbok, *Understanding the Holocaust*, p. 23.

Vienna between 1907 and 1913, listened to what people like these said.[1] But Russia also made really important contribution to the anti-Semitism of the period.

From the pogroms of the 1880s on, Jews in Russia experienced a concerted programme of often violent discrimination. An anti-Semitic group called the Black Hundreds was formed and favoured deporting Jews to the Arctic or Siberia. Some of its members also supported physical extermination.[2] It was also in Russia that a pamphlet called *The Protocols of the Elders of Zion* began to circulate. Apparently Tsar Nicholas II thought it was genuine, although subsequent historical analysis attributed it to the imperial secret police. *The Protocols* purported to be the minutes of a meeting held by Jewish leaders supposedly engaged in a conspiracy to enslave the world by secret means. The document suggested the Jews had almost shackled the states of Europe in 'unbreakable chains.'[3] *The Protocols* was important because by positing a world conspiracy to exploit Christians, it gave anti-Semites a reason to pursue their counter-mission on a global scale. The idea that the Jewish aim was almost achieved only added to anti-Semites' sense of urgency.

1.3 Hitler and Nazism

At the start of the twentieth century, it was not inevitable that a politician like Adolf Hitler would emerge to run Germany and it was hardly imaginable that an event such as the Holocaust would be pursued by a modern state system over a period of years. But neither was anti-Semitism negligible. It was as an undercurrent of mainstream society, even among educated classes. Symptomatically, during the First World War German military circles became so concerned about whether German Jews were fulfilling their duties to the Fatherland that in October 1916 a census was launched to investigate.[4]

Of course the period 1914 to 1918 was profoundly depressing as millions died on battlefields and whole societies reeled from the consequences of world war. Not only were there anti-Semitic pogroms in Ukraine, but up to 800,000 Christian Armenians died in the Ottoman Empire.[5] Germany's capitulation and the abdication of the Kaiser produced a particularly bleak mood in which Communists rebelled across the coun-

---

[1] B. Hamann, *Hitler's Vienna. A Dictator's Apprenticeship* (OUP, 1999), chapter 2.
[2] N. Cohn, *Warrant for Genocide. The Myth of the Jewish World-Conspiracy and the Protocols of the Elders of Zion*, (Chico, CA: Scholars Press, 1981), p. 112.
[3] Ibid, p. 263.
[4] Longerich, *Die Ermordung der Europäischen Juden*, p. 19.
[5] L. Kuper, *Genocide. Its Political Use in the Twentieth Century* (New Haven: Yale. 1981), chapter 6.

try. In Munich, a radical nationalist organisation called the Thule Society opposed the formation of a Soviet Republic there. It was attended by an émigré from the former Russian Empire called Alfred Rosenberg (1893–1946). Born in Tallinn (today, the capital of Estonia) he had fled the Baltic region as the German army retreated.[1] Later the ideological guru of National Socialism who wrote *The Myth of the Twentieth Century* (1930), Rosenberg introduced the Thule Society and those around it, such as Adolf Hitler, to *The Protocols*. He edited a copy of the tract and, like the Tsar, Hitler always believed the document to be true.[2] In this shady setting, the conspiratorial and biological strands of anti-Semitism were woven together into a battle of 'Good' against 'Evil.' Shortly before his execution after the Second World War, an SS war criminal explained what he thought had happened:

> A straight line leads from the *Protocols of the Elders of Zion* to Rosenberg's *Myth*. It is absolutely impossible to make any impression on this outlook by means of logical or rational argument, it is a sort of religiosity, and it impels people to form themselves into a sect. Under the influence of this literature millions of people believed these things—an event which can only be compared with similar phenomena in the Middle Ages, such as the witch-mania.
>
> Against this world of evil the race-mystics set the world of good, of light, incarnated in blond, blue-eye people, who were supposed to be the source of all capacity for creating civilization or building a state. Now these two worlds were alleged to be locked in a perpetual struggle, and the war of 1939, which Hitler unleashed, represented only the final battle between these two powers.[3]

Rosenberg stitched together pre-existing anti-Semitic ideas to create something new and Adolf Hitler did the same. His early speeches delivered in Munich's beer halls applied religious imagery and Bible stories to mock Jews.[4] *Mein Kampf* used pseudo-biological phrases to identify them as bearers of infection and to call for the purification of the nation's blood.[5] He too interpreted the struggle between races as a battle between everything noble in the world and everything despicable.[6] Hitler had

---

1 K. Heiden, *Der Fuehrer. Hitler's Rise to Power* (London: Victor Gollancz, 1944), pp. 21–3.
2 Cohn, *Warrant for Genocide* pp. 180–2.
3 Statement of SS Captain Dieter Wisliceny made before his execution in Czechoslovakia in November 1946. See Cohn, *Warrant for Genocide*, p. 180.
4 M. Housden, *Hitler. Study of a Revolutionary?* (London: Routledge, 2000), pp. 27–8.
5 A. Hitler, *Mein Kampf* (London: Hutchinson, 1985), p. 53.
6 Ibid, chapter 11 'Nation and Race.'

his own theory of Jewish conspiracy too. He said there was a six-phase historical process through which Jews were attempting to take over the international economy.[1]

With much good reason many historians have been dismissive of Nazi ideas. As Hans Mommsen says, they were 'neither consistent nor particularly original.' Racial ideology was 'an eclectic conglomeration of *völkisch* [i.e. radically nationalist] concepts indistinguishable from the programmes of out and out nationalist organisations' from the imperial period.[2] It is also true that the Nazi Party programme, proclaimed by Hitler on 24 February 1920, copied a great many of the principles of the German Workers' Party based in Nuremberg, for instance that Jews be excluded from public office.[3] For Martin Broszat, the Nazi Party was a chaotic, dishonest attempt to manipulate a desperate German electorate.[4] Mommsen agrees it was 'a negative people's party' which capitalised on the multiple dissatisfactions of the time.[5]

We should, however, keep these points in context. Hitler himself had been trained as an anti-Communist propagandist by the army after the war and he probably did try to use anti-Semitism as a rhetorical device to motivate his audiences—after all, political speeches are supposed to do just this. It is also true that less than 10% of Nazi Party members were attracted by specifically its anti-Semitism.[6] But none of this meant anti-Semitism was marginal for the likes of Rosenberg and Hitler. As Hans Mommsen acknowledges, Hitler really was a dyed in the wool anti-Semite who favoured the extermination of the Jews and other racial groups.[7]

Appropriately, then, Hitler tried to give his anti-Semitism new twists. In 1919 he said that persecution driven by emotion would only produce sporadic pogroms; concerted, 'rational' anti-Semitism, however, should withdraw legal privileges from Jews and then lead to their complete deportation.[8] He and his Party adapted anti-Semitism to the circumstances of the 1920s too. Ideas of an international conspiracy to enslave Germany were linked to international demands for reparations. The idea of

---

1   Housden, *Hitler*, p. 29.
2   H. Mommsen, 'National Socialism: Continuity and Change', in W. Lacqueur (ed.), *Fascism. A Reader's Guide* (London: Penguin, 1976), p. 152.
3   A. Tyrell, *Vom Trommler zum Führer*. Munich: Fink. 1975. p. 82.
4   M. Broszat, 'Die völkische Ideologie und der Nationalsozialismus', in *Deutsche Rundschau* 84 (1954) p. 55.
5   Mommsen, 'National Socialism', p. 154.
6   P. H. Merkl, *Political Violence under the Swastika* (Princeton, 1985), p. 453.
7   H. Mommsen, 'The Realization of the Unthinkable. The Final Solution and the Jewish Question in the Third Reich', in H. Mommsen (ed.), *From Weimar to Auschwitz* (Cambridge: Polity Press. 1991), p. 234.
8   W. Maser, *Hitler's Letters and Notes* (London: Heinemann, 1974), pp. 213–6.

a final economic crisis leading to global Jewish domination was linked to the onset of the Depression. And then there was Bolshevism. Since a number of famous Russian and German Bolsheviks (e.g. Leon Trotsky and Rosa Luxemburg respectively) had Jewish backgrounds, it was only a short step to saying that the spread of Communism was part of a single massive plot. Communism was presented as a ploy to set German against German in class war, to weaken the nation and leave it helpless in the face of Jewish infiltration.[1]

1.4 From 1933 to 1939

The Nazi Party has been described as uniquely unprepared for political power on 30 January 1933.[2] To this way of thinking, it lacked a proper political programme and never created a sensible system to generate new policies. Political decision-making primarily reflected the ambitions and rivalries of the individual paladins around Hitler. Consequently the gradual intensification of Jewish policy was an unintended consequence of this unrestrained and competitive political world, the 'cumulative radicalization' of persecution occurred for every reason other than ideological belief.[3] From this angle, Hitler promulgated the Nuremberg Laws in September 1935 not because he wanted to, but in response to pressure from the 'grass roots' of the Nazi Party for action on the Jewish Question. Likewise the vitriolic speech by Josef Goebbels which sparked 'Crystal Night' in November 1938 has been interpreted as an effort to gain status in the Führer's eyes relative to Hermann Göring.[4]

This reading of history contains a grain of truth. The Third Reich really was a chaotic place where different organisations fought each other to do the same job and where a gap often existed between policy planning and implementation. The environment did colour how policy emerged and what happened as a result, but we should not turn such factors into the decisive motor which first caused and then accelerated persecution between 1933 and 1939.

True, people did not flock to the Nazi Party specifically because of Hitler's anti-Semitism, but nor did it prevent them supporting him. It seems that roughly 20% of

---

1 Housden, *Hitler*, pp. 31–2.
2 Mommsen, 'National Socialism', p. 165.
3 H. Mommsen, 'Anti-Jewish Politics and the Implementation of the Holocaust', in H. Bull (ed.), *The Challenge of the Third Reich* (Oxford: Clarendon, 1986), p. 130.
4 See for instance the essay by U. D. Adam in W. H. Pehle (ed.), *November 1938* (Oxford: Berg, 1991).

early party members were attracted to the party by Hitler's style of leadership.[1] It is appropriate, therefore, that Ian Kershaw has tried to replace the idea of 'cumulative radicalisation' with 'working towards the Führer.'[2] This was the expectation that officials in the Hitler State should behave in ways the Führer would approve if he knew what was being done. Hitler's words, party documents and prior anti-Semitic materials had always been clear enough about the framework for a future Jewish policy. There were more than a few obvious steps that could be included in anti-Semitic politics: ban Jews from German citizenship, remove their civil rights, minimise their influence on public life, segregate them from 'proper' Germans, deport them and employ increasingly violent methods against them. Hitler's obvious belief in a global Jewish conspiracy which involved Bolshevism had to have consequences too.

In this light Hermann Graml is correct to say that that Jewish policy in the Third Reich grew up not as a chance consequence of political competition in a ruleless, chaotic environment, but involved the 'maturation and revelation of an essentially radical conviction.'[3] Even if the Third Reich lacked formal policy planning systems, nonetheless its participants were perfectly able to understand the principles of anti-Semitism and think through their consequences for themselves. So even if politicians and administrators wanted to compete with each other in the Third Reich, the rules of the 'game' of 'Jewish policy' were clear enough anyway. More or less in harmony with this view, Raul Hilberg said anti-Semitic policy passed through a number of phases which were initiated by 'signposts' (i.e. as opposed to decisive 'orders') coming from the Reich leadership. Nazi officials had to respond to these with initiative and imagination.[4] Hilberg's phases, incidentally, first involved the 'definition' of Jews, the 'expropriation' of their assets, 'concentration' of their living space and lastly their 'annihilation.'

Hermann Graml's later stage model of how Jewish policy developed is more sophisticated.[5] He says initially there was a phase called 'the reversal of emancipation' which lasted from the seizure of power until early 1935. Jews lost their civil rights, were dismissed from jobs in the civil service or the military, and experienced discrimination at school and university. Next came a period of 'isolation' when contact between Jews and Germans fell away. It began in May 1935 with a boycott of Jewish shops and included the Nuremberg Laws of September 1935 which deprived

---

1 P. H. Merkl, *Political Violence under the Swastika* (Princeton, 1985), p. 453.
2 I. Kershaw, *Hitler. 1889–1936. Hubris* (London: Allen Lane, 1999), p. 529.
3 H. Graml, 'The Genesis of the Final Solution', in Pehle (ed.), *November 1938*, p. 175.
4 R. Hilberg, *The Destruction of the European Jews* (New York: New Viewpoints, 1973), p. 18.
5 Graml, *Antisemitism in the Third Reich*.

Jews of citizenship and criminalised both marriage to and sexual relations with Gentiles.[1] Third was the stage of 'expropriation' when Jews were stripped of their assets and businesses. This ran from early 1937 until the 'Crystal Night' pogroms and reached a crescendo immediately after the disturbances when, on 12 November 1938, Hermann Göring fined Germany's Jews a billion Reichsmarks as compensation for the recent destruction. 'Approach to genocide' is Graml's name for the last phase before the start of the Holocaust. It lasted from 'Crystal Night' until the launching of Operation Barbarossa and saw increasing numbers of physical attacks against Jews supplemented by ever harsher anti-Semitic rhetoric. It included Hitler's speech to the Reichstag on 30 January 1939 which prophesied that if 'Jewish international financiers' provoked another war, the consequence would be 'the annihilation of the Jewish race in Europe.'[2]

Admittedly not everything about Graml's model works. Anti-Semitism did not develop in quite such a neat and tidy way. Even before the First World War, Jews had been excluded from various clubs (such as cycling clubs) in Austria.[3] In November 1932 the Prussian Ministry of the Interior had already issued an order preventing Jews from changing their names to make them seem more German.[4] Organised violence against Jews occurred on the streets from an early time, not least during the boycott of Jewish shops on 1 April 1933. Nonetheless, Graml does help underline how an initial prejudice grew when it failed to encounter any significant countervailing moral force. It shows how the behaviour of some Germans deteriorated as they realised there would be no serious repercussions for outrageous behaviour and gradually forgot about customary restraints on immoral conduct.[5] This is why Wolfgang Benz describes the period 1933 to 1941 as one in which German psychologies were prepared for what would come later.[6] Deluged by anti-Semitic propaganda and initiatives, Germans were habituated into understanding that Jews were victims waiting to happen.

Such a stage model also encourages us to remember that more than immedi-

---

1   The Nuremberg Laws were The Reich Citizenship Law and the Law for the Protection of German Blood and Honour.
2   Graml, *Antisemitism in the Third Reich*, p. 148.
3   Pulzer, *Rise of Political Anti-Semitism*, pp. 223–4.
4   Longerich (ed.), *Die Ermorderung der Europäischen Juden*, p. 28.
5   M. Wildt, 'The Boycott Campaign as an Arena of Collective Violence against Jews in Germany, 1933–1938', in D. Bankier and I. Gutman (eds.), *Nazi Europe and the Final Solution* (Jerusalem: Yad Vashem, 2003), p. 71.
6   W. Benz, 'Exclusion as a Stage in Persecution. The Jewish Situation in Germany, 1933–1941', in Bankier and Gutman (eds.), *Nazi Europe and the Final Solution*, p. 41.

ate expediency stood behind the various anti-Semitic initiatives of the Third Reich. Hitler may well have hoped to make a propaganda 'splash' when he proclaimed the Nuremberg Laws, but comparable legislation had been the subject of debate among doctors and lawyers for months beforehand.[1] Equally Avrahim Barkai shows that the exclusion of the Jews from Germany's economy that reached an apogee after 'Crystal Night' in fact had roots in economic decisions taken in 1936 which were implemented by degrees over the next two years.[2] The murder of a German diplomat in Paris by a Jew might have provided the opportunity for Goebbels to promote himself within the Reich by giving a rabid speech that signalled the start of the 'Crystal Night' riots, but the economic outcomes of the unrest had been a long time coming. In other words, longer term developments set the context for individual anti-Semitic actions, even if they seemed opportunistic at first sight.

1.5 Conclusion

It bears emphasis that after 1933 people began to buy in to anti-Semitism more wholeheartedly than was demanded by careerism and in-fighting alone. Only the gradual cultivation of a more positive attitude towards persecution could have motivated them to compel Jews to adopt the names 'Sara' or 'Israel' (thanks to a law of 17 August 1938) or ban them from sitting on park benches.[3] The developing caste of mind built on traditional anti-Semitism which went back centuries. In Germany in particular it had been re-discovered and re-invented in the late nineteenth century, at which time pseudo-scientific ideas were added to customary expressions of hatred. After the First World War, ideas of global Jewish conspiracy, imported from the former Russian Empire, joined the mixture. The Nazi Party popularised these ways of thinking and set the context for their exploitation and growth after the seizure of power in 1933.

---

1   Graml, *Antisemitism in the Third Reich*, p. 110.
2   A. Barkai, 'The Fateful Year 1938', in Pehle (ed.), *November 1938*, pp. 103–4.
3   M. Burleigh and W. Wippermann, *The Racial State. Germany 1933–1945* (CUP, 1993), pp. 85–87.

Chapter 2 The Pursuit of the Holocaust

2.1 Introduction

Moving from an understanding of the Holocaust's background to an uncontroversial explanation of how exactly the event came about is a deceptively tricky business. At critical points we lack decisive evidence and so it is hard to pin down the exact process of decision-making which took place at the head of the Reich in spring and summer 1941. We just don't know what happened in, say, private talks between Hitler and Himmler held at this time. The commandant of Auschwitz, Rudolf Höss, could not remember precisely when he met Hitler for an important discussion. Members of the *Einsatzgruppen* gave different accounts of when they were told to kill every single Jew in the East.[1] Sometimes we seem to have been left with more questions than answers. What was Hitler's specific role in launching the genocide? On which dates were important decisions taken and key orders given? What was the relationship between the Holocaust and the war in the East? And did events grow by 'quantum leaps' or gradual steps?

What's more, although it is easy to see that a great deal about the Holocaust was unique, not least its extermination camps and industrialised killing methods, still we have to think about the relationship between this attempted genocide and other policies in the Third Reich. Under cover of war, extensive operations were begun to murder mentally dysfunctional Germans, not to say members of the Sinti and Roma.[2] There were plans to destroy the Polish nation, indeed massive projects were started to reconstruct the entire population between Germany and the Urals. A proper explanation of the Holocaust also needs to take into account its connections to these wider political goals.

---

1   For Höss's inexact memory, see W. Benz, *Der Holocaust* (Munich: C.H. Beck, 1995), pp. 102–3. For trouble with testimony from members of the *Einsatzgruppen*, see A. Streim, 'The Tasks of the Einsatzgruppen', in *Simon Wiesenthal Centre Annual* 4 (1987) pp. 309–28.
2   On 1 November 1941 it was reported that troops preferred shooting Jews to gypsies because the latter made too much fuss.

2.2   1939–1940: Feeling the way

On 30 January 1939, not long after 'Crystal Night,' Hitler delivered a speech to the Reichstag. He mentioned the Jewish Question briefly but unambiguously:

> I said that I would one day take over the leadership of the state, and with it that of the whole nation, and that I would then among many other things settle the Jewish problem.... Today I will once more be a prophet: if the international Jewish financiers in and outside Europe should succeed in plunging the nations once more into a world war, then the result will not be the bolshevization of the earth, and thus the victory of Jewry, but the annihilation of the Jewish race in Europe![1]

As war drew closer, the Führer's rhetoric extended beyond Europe's Jews. On 22 August 1939 he told Germany's military chiefs the following:

> Our strength is our quickness and our brutality. Genghis Kahn had millions of women and children killed by his own will and with a gay heart. History sees only in him a great state builder.... Thus for the time-being I have sent to the East only my "Death's Head Units" with the order to kill without pity or mercy all men, women and children of Polish race or language. Only in such a way will we win vital space that we need. Who still talks nowadays of the extermination of the Armenians?[2]

War had been on Hitler's mind for some time. Preparation for conflict stood behind the introduction of the Four Year Plan in 1936. The Hossbach Memorandum shows that in November 1937 he was thinking about when best to start a conflict. But the way Hitler spoke in 1939 indicated this would be a fight unlike any other in modern times. From the outset Hitler was threatening the commission of atrocities and genocide.

The German army which invaded Poland on 1 September 1939 was followed by six units of security police. On 25 August 1939 they had been instructed to implement Operation Tannenberg which involved trying to murder 3% of the Polish population, especially members of the intelligentsia. The aim was to eradicate potential Polish leaders and to destroy the very idea of their nation. This operation also provided an opportunity to get rid of members of other 'undesirable' population groups (like

---

1   N. N. Baynes (ed.), *The Speeches of Adolf Hitler. Volume 1* (OUP, 1942), p. 741.
2   Quoted in R. Breitman, *The Architect of Genocide. Himmler and the Final Solution* (London: Bodley Head, 1991), p. 43.

Jews) and massacres followed.[1] The action was so appalling that senior military men such as General Blaskowitz complained to Hitler. As a result Blaskowitz was later relieved of his duties as commander in chief in the East.[2]

Even before the end of September 1939, on their own initiative some Nazi leaders in occupied Poland began shooting patients in mental asylums so they could use the hospitals as barracks. In fact many German leaders understood the war to be a perfect chance to 'get away' with things they could not otherwise have done. The idea of killing people with severe mental dysfunction was not new, but in summer 1939 Hitler had commissioned officials to start planning actually to do this. It was decided that between 65,000 and 70,000 people would be subjected to 'euthanasia' in an operation which became known as 'T-4' after the Berlin address of the project's head offices at '*Tiergartenstrasse 4.*' In October 1939 Hitler issued a written order authorising the euthanasia of individuals with incurable conditions.[3] As a result, men like Viktor Brack and Christian Wirth set about developing appropriate killing methods which later would find a different application.

Meanwhile speedy military victory in Poland was raising the question of what exactly the Nazi leadership was going to do with the newly captured territories. On 6 October 1939 Hitler went public on this score. He told the Reichstag there needed to be a racial 'cleansing effort' to create 'a new order of ethnographic relationships' in the East.[4] Whole population groups were to be moved. The idea should not have been completely unexpected. In the early 1930s Hitler had suggested moving the Czech nation to Siberia to make more space for Germans and in the years before the war, one or two (admittedly marginal) Nazi offices had begun planning for a new racial ordering or Europe.[5] The day after his Reichstag speech, however, Hitler appointed *Reichsführer-SS* Heinrich Himmler Reich Commissioner for the Consolidation of the German Nation. As such, his commission included the repatriation of German communities from around the continent,[6] the creation of new communities of Germans and the removal of 'harmful' population groups. In other words, the German nation

---

1 M. Housden, *Hans Frank: Lebensraum and the Holocaust* (Basingstoke: Palgrave, 2003), pp. 116–8.
2 S. Haffner, *The Meaning of Hitler* (London: Weidenfeld and Nicolson, 1988), p. 135.
3 M. Burleigh and W. Wippermann, *The Racial State. Germany 1933–1945* (CUP, 1993), pp. 147–8. More fully, see chapter 6. Also J. Noakes and G. Pridham (eds.), *Nazism 1919–1945. Volume 3. Foreign Policy, War and Racial Extermination* (Exeter University Press, 1988), chapter 36.
4 M. Broszat, *Zweihundert Jahre deutsche Polenpolitik* (Munich: Suhrkamp, 1972), p. 277.
5 H. Rauschning, *Hitler Speaks* (London: Thornton Butterworth, 1939), pp. 40–7.
6 German communities existed in, for instance, France, the Baltic States, Hungary, Czechoslovakia, Yugoslavia and the Volga Valley in Russia.

was to be brought together and strengthened, while other nationalities were to be ejected from their midst.

The manipulation of whole populations was ambitious, but actually it was underway already when the Führer addressed the Reichstag. As early as 29 September 1939, Hitler had told Alfred Rosenberg that he wanted occupied Poland divided into three strips. The western-most territories were to be incorporated into Germany (as they had been before 1914), Poles would live in the middle, and Jews would be settled in the eastern-most section (between the rivers Bug and Vistula).[1] Already on 21 September, Reinhard Heydrich, head of the Reich Security Head Office and right-hand man to Heinrich Himmler, had ordered that Jews in occupied Poland be gathered together in ghettos close to railway stations. He wanted them 'resettled' swiftly from the western-most territories towards the east—to lands which became part of the Government General led by the long-standing Nazi Hans Frank. Four days later, Himmler ordered the movement to start. Next month Adolf Eichmann, an SS specialist in Jewish emigration who worked in the Reich Security Head Office, began to plan the transfer of 550,000 Jews. The undertaking was supposed to be completed by February 1940.[2]

The so-called 'Nisko project' was expected to be horrible. Its victims were being sent to an inhospitable part of Poland in the depths of winter and preparations to receive them were minimal. The Nazis involved understood that many would die as a consequence.[3] As it turned out, however, 'Nisko' was a fiasco. True, some transportations did occur. For instance, in December 1939 87,000 Jews were moved from around Posen (today Poznan) to the Government General. But things were done so chaotically that Governor General Hans Frank began complaining that 'Nisko' was upsetting the war economy. In February 1940 he was backed up by the head of the Four Year Plan, Hermann Göring, and so Hitler halted the plan.

This left Himmler with a problem. He had begun supervising the transfer of ethnic German communities to Nazi-occupied territory from around Eastern Europe, for instance from the Baltic States which were now being occupied by the Soviet Union. The Germans were being housed temporarily in the Polish territories incorporated into the Reich, such as *Warthegau*. Their new homes included the now vacant asy-

---

1   P. Burrin, *Hitler and the Jews. The Genesis of the Holocaust* (London: Edward Arnold, 1994), pp. 69-70.
2   M. Housden, *Hans Frank. Lebensraum and the Holocaust* (Basingstoke: Palgrave, 2003), p. 132.
3   G. Aly, *Final Solution. Nazi Population Policy and the Murder of the European Jews* (London: Arnold, 1999), pp. 17–8.

lums and properties from which Jews and Poles had been removed. But more and more ethnic Germans kept arriving in the incorporated territories even though the Government General refused to accept any more Jews and Poles from the region. As a result, SS officials in the likes of *Warthegau* faced increasing problems of overcrowding in respect of both ethnic Germans and, of course, Jews and Poles. There was a log-jam of people and gradually the situation developed into a real headache.

Some argue that even at this early point the straightforward physical eradication of Europe's Jews was a serious policy possibility. For instance, in his order of 21 September Reinhard Heydrich distinguished a 'final aim' for the removal of Jews from 'the stages leading to the fulfilment of this final aim.'[1] Herman Graml thinks this 'can only be understood as an intention to exterminate the Jews which was to be realized in the near future.'[2] We have to be a little careful here, however. For example, in early 1940 Himmler described 'the Bolshevist method of the physical destruction of a people' as 'un-German and impossible.'[3] Despite the difficulties associated with the 'Nisko' project, during 1939 and 1940 'resettlement' (albeit of a kind likely to cause multiple deaths) was, in practice, the order of the day. In this context, Madagascar came on the menu.

To Richard Breitman's mind, the crisis over what to do with especially Jews who could not be moved from the likes of *Warthegau* to the Government General created the need for 'an imaginary goal' which gave officials the hope that their mounting problems over resettlement would be solved sooner or later.[4] But the Madagascar plan was more than just a diversion from a difficult reality. Before the Second World War there had been international discussions (for instance at the Évian conference in 1938) of whether Germany's Jews could be offered safe haven at various locations around the globe. Officials from Poland even suggested specifically Madagascar as a home for 2,000 to 60,000 people.[5] Perhaps the thinking inspired Franz Rademacher, a member of the German Foreign Office, because in June 1940 he recommended that the peace treaty with France transfer Madagascar to German control. He wanted 25,000 French citizens to be replaced by four million Jews who would be shipped from Europe once general peace was declared. Thereafter they would administer their own affairs as supervised by the SS.

---

1 Y. Arad, I. Gutman and A. Margaliot (eds.), *Documents on the Holocaust* (Jerusalem: Yad Vashem, 1996), p. 173.
2 H. Graml, *Antisemitism in the Third Reich* (Oxford: Blackwell, 1992), p. 154.
3 Breitman, *Architect of Genocide*, pp. 118–9.
4 Ibid, p. 138.
5 Benz, *Der Holocaust*, p. 53.

At the time, a number of important Nazis seemed to take the idea seriously. According to Adolf Eichmann, this was true of the Reich Security Head Office.[1] Madagascar was also mentioned in Governor General Frank's public speeches and, in anticipation of Jews being removed from Europe, work on the ghettos in his territory was halted.[2] Magnus Brechtken doubts, however, that Hitler personally was so enthusiastic.[3] Although he discussed Madagascar with German figures and some foreign dignitaries, Brechtken says Hitler did nothing to promote the scheme. Brechtken insists that even now he was set on the genocide of Europe's Jews and goes on to argue that deportation to the harsh climate of the tropics would have amounted to a death sentence as complete as a trip to the gas chambers of Auschwitz.[4] Even if Brechtken might exaggerate a little here, he does highlight how things were developing at the head of the Reich. Resettlement to Nisko had been expected to cause many Jews to die and (if taken seriously) relocation to far-distant Madagascar surely would have produced an even worse outcome. In other words, the gap between 'resettling' Europe's Jews and their direct physical annihilation was becoming less and less significant.

The trend continued during the next winter. On Hitler's orders, there were fresh attempts between November 1940 and March 1941 to transport Jews from the Reich to the Government General. Once again they failed. At the same time, Nazi eyes began looking towards a military campaign with Russia. On 4 December 1940 Himmler wrote about sending the Jews to a 'territory yet to be determined' and a fortnight later Hitler commissioned Operation Barbarossa.[5] Now ideas circulated about dispatching Jews to frozen wastes further to the East (even to Siberia) where they would be used as disposable slave labourers. They might, for instance, drain marshes or dig a canal. Given the inevitability of work being carried out under SS supervision and in horrendous conditions, these ideas did amount to plans to exterminate large numbers of people.

Meanwhile conditions facing Nazi resettlement administrators were not improving. Ethnic Germans were still in temporary camps in *Warthegau*. Large numbers of Jews were still in Polish ghettos. Łódź ghetto had been closed in May 1940 and

---

1   H. Arendt, *Eichmann in Jerusalem. A Report on the Banality of Evil* (London: Penguin, 1994), p. 78.
2   M. Brechtken, *Madagaskar für die Juden. Antisemitische Idee und politische Praxis 1885–1945* (Munich: Oldenburg, 1998), p. 238.
3   Ibid, p. 271.
4   Ibid, p. 295.
5   Aly, *Final Solution*, p. 196.

Warsaw in November. Cracow and Lublin followed suit in March 1941. Conditions here were deteriorating constantly as cold, hunger and typhus produced high mortality rates throughout the winter.[1] The situation led *SS-Sturmbannführer* Höppner to send a memorandum to Adolf Eichmann on 16 July 1941. Nervous of the consequences of what was happening in the ghettos he said:

> There is a danger that, in the coming winter, it will become impossible to feed all the Jews. It must seriously be considered whether the most humane solution is to finish off the Jews unfit for labour through some fast-acting means. This would definitely be more pleasant than letting them starve to death.[2]

The comments came just three weeks after Hitler had launched his invasion of the Soviet Union.

2.3 1941: A new mood

Operation Barbarossa began on 22 June 1941. The event certainly helped promote the right psychological conditions for the physical destruction of Europe's Jews as 'a thing in itself' rather than as the by-product of resettlement or hard labour.[3] It was planned and implemented during a period marked by a new severity which complemented Höppner's thinking too. Once again speeches by Hitler set the tone. On 30 March 1941 he told over 200 senior military men they were about to see a 'battle of annihilation' in which Communist officials and intellectuals would be exterminated.[4] Correspondingly on 13 May 1941 the Jurisdiction Order was circulated among the military which exonerated soldiers in advance for any crime committed during the forthcoming invasion. Most infamous of all, however, was the Commissar Order of 6 June 1941 which authorised the murder of all Soviet Communist Party officials.

The steps reflected Hitler's belief that Communism was a Jewish phenomenon and that the invasion of Russia was going to be a more radical racial event than even the attack on Poland. Predictably then (and despite the lack of success up to that point), new plans began to be drawn up to re-shape Europe's population. Following

---

1 See C. R. Browning, *The Path to Genocide* (CUP, 1992), chapter 2.
2 Quoted in Aly, *Final Solution*, p. 214.
3 O. Bartov, 'Operation Barbarossa and the Origins of the Final Solution', in D. Cesarani (ed.), *The Final Solution. Origins and Implementation* (London: Routledge, 1994), p. 120.
4 H. A. Jacobsen (ed.), *Generaloberst Halder. Kriegstagebuch. Band II. Von der geplanten Landung in England bis zum Beginn des Ostfeldzuges. (1.7.1940–21.6.1941)* (Stuttgart: W. Kohlhammer Verlag, 1963), pp. 336–7

meetings with Hitler and Himmler, on 25 March 1941 Governor General Hans Frank declared that in 15 to 20 years his territory would be completely free of Jews and Poles. These 12 million people would be replaced by 4 to 5 million Germans, making his territory as German as the Rhineland. On 1 April he explained that, according to Hitler, the Government General would be the first area cleared of its Jews.[1] This was also a period when Hermann Göring expected 20 to 30 million people to die during the Russian campaign and when Heinrich Himmler commissioned a report called General Plan East which outlined the reconstruction of Europe's population as far as the Urals.[2] In due course Himmler's plans foresaw 31 million non-Germans being removed to Siberia over a 30 year period. They would be replaced by 10 million Germans

Spring 1941 also saw the establishment of special action police units (*Einsatzgruppen*) to act behind advancing military troops. Initially they comprised 3,000 men and were led by very well qualified people, including doctors of law. They were divided into 4 units—A, B, C and D—and their terms of reference were defined in an order of 13 March:[3]

> the *Reichsführer-SS* has been given by the Führer certain special tasks within the operations zone of the army; these stem from the necessity finally to settle the conflict between two opposing political systems. Within the framework of these tasks the *Reichsführer-SS* will act independently and on his own responsibility.[4]

Just as there has been debate about the exact significance of resettlement projects, so there have been arguments about whether the *Einsatzgruppen* were the first agents of the Holocaust. This might seem odd given that between June 1941 and April 1942 they killed 560,000 people (including almost the entire Jewish population) in the invaded territories.[5] Discussion, however, has revolved around the precise orders given to them just before they advanced into occupied territory. After the war Otto Ohlendorf, leader of *Einsatzgruppe D*, said they were ordered verbally to destroy every single Jew they found. Others, however, have maintained that an order for total killing came only later. Alfred Streim, for instance, says Ohlendorf's evidence

---

1 Housden, *Hans Frank*, p. 142.
2 Aly, *Final Solution*, p. 186.
3 'A' operated in the Baltic, 'B' in White Russia, 'C' in Ukraine and 'D' in the Crimea.
4 Quoted in H. Krausnick and M. Broszat, *Anatomy of the SS State* (London: Paladin, 1982), p. 78.
5 Benz, *Holocaust*, p. 60.

is unreliable because he was trying to suggest that when he killed people in the East, he was 'only following orders.'[1] So what can we say for certain about the actions of these special units?

Once Operation Barbarossa began, every single Jew in the conquered territories became a potential victim of the *Einsatzgruppen*. This reflected the nature of their work. On 17 June 1941, Head of the Reich Security Head Office Reinhard Heydrich ordered that the units stimulate anti-Semitic pogroms by local populations. The message was repeated in a letter written by Heydrich on 29 June and in one from Himmler to senior SS leaders dated 2 July 1941. The *Einsatzgruppen* embarked on their work quickly. In the Baltic States *Einsatzgruppe A*, led by Walther Stahlecker, shot Jews themselves on 24 June in Garzdai, Lithuania. On the night of 25-26 June, however, they opened the prisons of Kaunas (also in Lithuania) and encouraged former inmates to attack the local Jewish community. 1,500 people were killed as a result. *Einsatzgruppe C* was deployed to Ukraine where pogroms hit 58 communities and accounted for tens of thousands of lives during the same summer.[2]

Pogroms actually proved easier to instigate in some places than others. Sometimes Lithuanians began to kill Jews even before the Germans arrived.[3] In fact 95% of Lithuania's Jews died during the Second World War and over half were killed by Lithuanians.[4] In Latvia, however, the local population required more encouragement by German authorities. In the end, however, a local collaborator, Viktors Arajs, set up a militia which murdered between 26,000 and 60,000 people, including very many Jews.[5] Collaborationist groups assisting the *Einsatzgruppen* were formed in the Ukraine under the nationalist Yaroslav Stetsko.

The *Einsatzgruppen* received support from the *Wehrmacht*. Without this, just 3,000 men would never have achieved all that they did across so vast an area as the

---

1 Streim, 'The Tasks of the Einsatzgruppen', pp. 309–28.
2 S. S. Friedman, *A History of the Holocaust* (London: Valentine Mitchell, 2004), p. 182 and 187. C. Dieckmann, 'Der Krieg und die Ermordung der litauischen Juden', in U. Herbert (ed.), *Nationalsozialistische Vernichtungspolitik 1939–1945* (Frankfurt am Main: Fischer, 1998), p. 292.
3 A readily available study of the Holocaust in Lithuania during 1941 is provided by J. Tauber. '"Jews, your History on Lithuanian Soil is over!"' which can be found in the free access internet journal *Central and Eastern European Review* 1 (2007). www.ceer.org.uk. See also M. Greenbaum, *The Jews of Lithuania. A History of a Remarkable Community 1316–1945* (Jerusalem: Gefen, 1995), p. 307.
4 D. Porat, 'The Holocaust in Lithuania', in Cesarani (ed.), *Final Solution*, p. 163. Also V. Bartusevicius, W. Wette and J. Tauber (eds.), *Holocaust in Litauen: Krieg, Judenmord und Kollaboration* (Cologne: Boehlau Verlag, 2003).
5 A. Ezergailis, *The Holocaust in Latvia 1941–1944* (Riga: The Historical Institute of Latvia, 1996), chapter 6.

occupied East. So, for example, in July 1941 an infantry division helped eradicate Jews in the White Russian towns of Baranovichi and Novogrudok. In Ukraine, infantry units helped kill 1,160 Jews at Luck and military police assisted in the execution of 2,200 Jews at Gorky. As German troops entered eastern Galicia, they distributed leaflets telling the local populations to eliminate Jews.[1]

2.4 Garden of Eden

The mass killing of Jews was underway from the very outset of Operation Barbarossa, but it is also clear that something important happened between mid-July and early August 1941. The evidence can be found in reports compiled by the special action units themselves. One document says that between 22 July and 3 August 1941 *Einsatzkommando 3* (a section of an *Einsatzgruppe A*) executed 1,592 people, of whom 1,349 were men and 172 women.[2] On the single day of 12 September, however, they shot 3,334 people, of whom 993 were men, 1,670 women and 771 children. Before the end of the month they carried out another 7 actions and killed over 10,000 Jews.[3] So it seems that between July and September there was a change in how the *Einsatzgruppen* did their job. Overall their killings increased and they also included more women and children. Christopher Browning also notes that at the same time Heinrich Himmler began to make available thousands more men for this kind of work. On 23 July he allocated an additional 11 police battalions, roughly 6,000 men. By the end of the year, 33,000 men staffed comparable units.[4]

These developments have been interpreted as an important step on the way to the Holocaust. They have been viewed as the point at which the Nazi system switched from exterminating Jews who posed a military threat to the Third Reich (i.e. adult males), to exterminating absolutely all Jews in Hitler's new empire. Christopher Browning has argued that, expecting a speedy victory in the Soviet Union, on 16 July 1941 Hitler told senior government figures that it was time to create a 'Garden of Eden' in which the Crimea, Galicia, the Baltic, the Volga and Baku would all be included under German control. Browning indicates that there would have been no place at all for Jews in this 'garden.'[5] So either this speech, or some contemporaneous development associated with it, precipitated a heightened killing effort which

---

1 Friedman, *History of the Holocaust*, pp. 183–5.
2 Browning, *Path to Genocide*, p. 102, note 38.
3 Arad, Gutman and Margaliot (eds.), *Documents on the Holocaust*, p. 399.
4 C. R. Browning, 'Hitler and the Euphoria of Victory', in Cesarani (ed.), *Final Solution*, p. 140.
5 Browning, *Path to Genocide*, pp. 104–5.

amounted to the start of the Holocaust.

There are other hints that something important was happening at about this point. Rudolf Höss was commandant of Auschwitz concentration camp. In his post-war memoirs, he recalled that at some point over the summer (he could not remember when exactly) he met Hitler and was told he would have a central role in the Final Solution of the Jewish Question.[1] Also relevant is Hermann Göring's well-known memorandum of 13 July written to Reinhard Heydrich. It commissioned the chief of the Reich Security Head Office to solve the Jewish problem 'by emigration and evacuation in the most favourable way possible.' Göring wanted 'a complete solution of the Jewish Question in the German sphere of influence in Europe' and requested that appropriate plans be drawn up.[2] Given what the *Einsatzgruppen* were doing at the time, what must Göring's communication have meant really?

In the following months, unforgettable atrocities were committed. On 24 September an explosion shook Kiev and its local German military commander authorised reprisals against the civilian population. As a result specifically Jews were ordered to report to the crossroads of Melnikov and Dokhturov streets on 29 September. They were marched to a cemetery just outside the city at a place called Babi Yar where they were told to sit down and leave their belongings. Then, in groups of twenty to fifty, they were marched to the edge of a ravine where they were shot with a machine gun. Afterwards army engineers blew up the rocky cliff face to cover the bodies. 33,771 people died in this way.[3]

At about the same time, preparations began to send Jews from Western Europe to the killing fields in the East. Burrin has suggested that this move marked another escalation in Hitler's Jewish policy. He maintains that until this point murder was only in store for Eastern European Jews. But, since it was now clear that the Soviet Union would not be defeated before winter, the Führer became frustrated and decided to accelerate the murder of *all* Europe's Jews. Consequently on 18 September 1941 Himmler wrote to a *Gauleiter* in the East saying that Hitler wanted the Reich to be free of Jews as quickly as possible and in November deportations from Germany and Austria began to Riga and Minsk.[4] Within months, those arriving at Riga began simply to be shot. Further deportations soon began from occupied western territories such as France.

Obviously by the start of 1942 deportation amounted to a death sentence. For

---
1 See Benz, *Der Holocaust*, p. 102.
2 B. Sax and D. Kuntz (eds.), *Inside Hitler's Germany* (Lexington, Mass.: D.C.Heath, 1992), p. 433.
3 Friedman, *History of the Holocaust*, pp. 184–5.
4 P. Burrin, *Hitler and the Jews. The Genesis of the Holocaust* (London: Edward Arnold, 1994), p. 122 and 133.

Nazi administrators, however, it must have offered a way out of an increasingly difficult general resettlement situation. The invasion of the East had given the Third Reich more Jews than ever to deal with, Siberia obviously was impossible as a resettlement site and conditions in the ghettos were deteriorating continually.[1] One report noted that 898 people died in the Warsaw ghetto in January 1941, but 5,560 in August 1942.[2] In addition there was still the problem of ethnic Germans languishing in transit camps and awaiting re-location. These were extreme times and they would certainly witness extreme measures.

2.5 The technology of mass murder

1942 was a year of rather different transitions. As military operations first wavered and then became bogged down at Stalingrad, Himmler's racial projects moved into full swing. Before the Holocaust could become a complete reality, however, a number of problems had to be solved. Not least, it was clear that a properly adequate method of killing so very many people had to be found. Himmler himself was well aware that shooting large numbers was a gruesome business. When he personally witnessed a mass shooting near Minsk in August 1941 he was sick and almost fainted. There had to be a better way.

While war raged, inside the Third Reich 'T-4' had progressed swiftly. By summer 1941 between 60,000 and 70,000 mentally dysfunctional people had been killed. It was inevitable that so many deaths eventually would raise suspicions about what was happening, and on 3 August 1941 Cardinal August von Galen, Bishop of Münster, gave a sermon denouncing euthanasia.[3] The following uproar led Hitler to halt the operation. But the euthanasia project was important. In the first place it had encouraged thinking about how best to kill relatively large numbers of people efficiently. When lethal injections proved too slow, on 4 January 1940 euthanasia staff at an asylum near Berlin killed patients by pumping carbon monoxide into a room like a shower room.[4] Meanwhile, pursuing euthanasia at Polish asylums, in December 1939 and January 1940 SS officer Herbert Lange experimented with ways to gas mental

---

1. Nazi leaders themselves understood these sort of points. Hans Frank and Alfred Rosenberg discussed resettlement and Siberia, for instance, in mid-October 1941. Housden, *Hans Frank*, p. 150.
2. Arad, Gutman and Margaliot (eds), *Documents on the Holocaust*, p. 245.
3. Noakes and Pridham (ed.), *Nazism 1919–1945*, pp. 1036–40.
4. Noakes and Pridham (ed.), *Nazism 1919–1945*, pp. 1019–20. Burleigh and Wipperman, *Racial State,* chapter 6.

patients by funnelling exhaust fumes into the back of a sealed van. So, with their euthanasia work finished, what were such staff experienced in delivering death going to do now?

Burrin believes that if discussions took place over how industrialised mass murder should happen, they occurred in the first two weeks of October 1941.[1] But some critical decisions probably were taken more quickly even than this, not least because large numbers of euthanasia staff were deployed to the East with remarkable speed. Many went to work for Senior *SS-Führer* Odilo Globocnik who was chief of police in the Lublin region of the Government General. He controlled the extermination camps of Treblinka, Bełżec and Sobibór (Majdanek was in Lublin but fell to a different authority). In 1942 he led 'Operation Reinhard' to exterminate all the Jews of the Government General. Christian Wirth was one of 92 former-euthanasia employees who became involved in Operation Reinhard. Specifically he became Globocnik's 'Inspector of Camps.' Franz Stangl, also a participant in T-4, served as commandant of Sobibór and Treblinka.[2] Meanwhile, beyond the Government General and Globocnik's chain of command, Lange set up gassing installations for Jews and gypsies near Chełmno.[3] Gas vans were also used by the *Einsatzgruppen* in November and December 1941 in Ukraine before being deployed more generally during summer 1942.[4]

Experimental carbon monoxide gas chambers began to function near Moghilev (Ukraine) in September 1941 and carbon monoxide vans began operating at Chełmno on 8 December 1941. Tests were already underway, however, to find an even more efficient medium for murder. On 3 September 1941, 900 Soviet prisoners of war in Rudolf Höss's Auschwitz camp were gassed using the fumigating agent Zyklon-B. The experiment was a 'success' and next month discussions were begun there about the construction of crematoria with appropriate capacities.

2.6 Wannsee and beyond.

It is still shocking to understand that a whole modern organisation was involved in the development, management and eventual implementation of industrialised genocide. Gassing methods were researched, camps to hold victims were built, transport sys-

---
[1] Burrin, *Hitler and the Jews*, p. 231.
[2] Noakes and Pridham (eds), *Nazism 1919–1945*, pp. 1156. G. Sereny, *Into that Darkness* (London: Vintage, 1983).
[3] H. Friedlander, 'Euthanasia and the Final Solution', in Cesarani (ed.), *Final Solution*, pp. 54–5.
[4] Friedman, *History of the Holocaust*, p. 193.

tems to move them around were timetabled, and crematoria to dispose of the bodies were planned. Personnel had acquired necessary skills and were deployed to appropriate locations. A whole bureaucratic system was being built up for mass murder and everyone around it was sucked into events. On 16 December 1941 Hans Frank addressed a meeting of senior administrative personnel in the Government General. Only some belonged to the SS (Frank himself did not), but he told everyone present the following:

> One way or another ... we must finish off the Jews.... I will therefore, on principle, approach Jewish affairs in the expectation that the Jews will disappear.... We must destroy the Jews wherever we find them, and wherever it is possible, in order to maintain the whole structure of the Reich.... We cannot shoot these 3.5 million Jews [i.e. all the Jews in the Government General], we cannot poison them, but we will have to take measures that will lead somehow to [their] successful destruction.[1]

Organisations and their operations take a lot of controlling and it was imperative that a whole system dedicated to exterminating millions of people should run smoothly and without drawing more attention to itself than necessary. Problems with earlier resettlement projects had taught SS authorities that all administrative branches of the Third Reich had to co-operate or else there would be chaos. Consequently chief of the Reich Security Head Office Reinhard Heydrich called a meeting of senior officials from all interested Reich organisations. Originally scheduled for 9 December 1941, it was postponed until 20 January 1942. On that day officials from the Ministries of the Occupied East, the Interior and Justice, staff from the Government General and the Office of the Four Year Plan, from the Foreign Office, and the Reich Chancellery all met in a committee chaired by Heydrich and minuted by Adolf Eichmann. Just by calling this group together, Heydrich was letting everyone know that he was running the show and would tolerate no disruption to it.

This was the Wannsee conference, so-called because it took place in a large house (address Am Grossen Wannsee 56–58) on the banks of the lake bearing the same name.[2] Heydrich began by emphasising that Göring had commissioned him to prepare the 'Final Solution of the European Jewish Question' and said that the meeting was intended to clarify a number of points. Not least, he stressed that the matter fell entirely to the SS. As he recorded what unfolded, Eichmann used words carefully.

---

1 Quoted in Arad, Gutman and Margaliot (eds.), *Documents on the Holocaust*, pp. 247–9.
2 The house still exists. It is now a museum to the conference.

He did not write down terms like 'extermination' or 'gassing,' rather there would be 'evacuation of the Jews to the East' where labour under harsh conditions would cause large numbers of them to 'disappear through natural diminution.' It was estimated that eleven million people would to be affected.[1] This was bad enough, but the reality of what was being planned stood behind even minutes like these. Given that mass murder that was under way already, most Jews going to the East would not be worked to death, they would be killed outright.

In the wake of Wannsee and as spring approached, the main extermination camps in the East began to operate. The basic killing process involved people being crushed into supposed shower rooms before carbon monoxide (later Zyklon-B gas) was introduced from above. In about half an hour everyone was dead. In due course the gas was pumped out and the bodies were removed for cremation or disposal in mass graves. In Lublin, the south eastern area of the Government General where Odilo Globocnik was posted, the first dedicated extermination camp using gas chambers began to work at Bełżec on 17 March 1942. Another was started at Sobibór (also in Lublin) a few weeks after. Later in the year killing facilities were developed at Majdanek, also in the Government General. Auschwitz, located Upper Silesia (a territory incorporated into the Reich after the 1939 campaign) began operating the same spring, first killing Jews from the region and then occupied Europe as a whole.[2]

The murderous process went ahead in fits and starts. On 19 July 1942, Himmler ordered Globocnik to exterminate all of the Jews in the Government General who were incapable of work. Subsequent events, which included the 'clearing' of all the ghettos in the Government General, were called 'Operation Reinhard' after Reinhard Heydrich who was assassinated in Prague in early June. Globocnik led the proceedings and developed a new extermination facility at Treblinka which killed over a quarter of a million people in its first month of operation. This camp, plus Bełżec and Sobibór, accounted for the lives of about a million people over the next year.[3] As Operation Reinhard neared its end, in November 1943 they were dismantled and the remaining Jews were shot.[4]

---

1   For minutes of the meeting, see Sax and Kuntz (eds.), *Inside Hitler's Germany*, pp. 433-41. Discussions of the meeting can be found in M. Roseman, *The Villa, the Lake, the Meeting. Wannsee and the Final Solution* (London: Penguin, 2003) and Benz, *Der Holocaust*, chapter 1.

2   Y. Gutman, 'Auschwitz—an Overview', in Y. Gutman and M. Berenbaum (eds.), *Anatomy of the Auschwitz Death Camp* (Bloomington: Indiana University Press, 1998).

3   Noakes and Pridham (eds), *Nazism 1919–1945*, p. 1156. For a detailed study of the camps at the centre of Operation Reinhard, see Y. Arad, *Belzec, Sobibor, Treblinka. The Operation Reinhard Death Camps* (Bloomington: Indiana University Press, 1987).

4   These people were killed despite working in armaments factories. The initiative disrupted muni-

Jews were transported to killing sites from locations all around occupied Europe. Deportations from occupied France to Auschwitz started in March 1942. In autumn deportations were organised from Belgium and the Netherlands. Even after the military failure at Stalingrad, the exterminatory project went ahead at pace. The Jews of Salonika were deported to Auschwitz in spring 1943 and Jewish communities in Hungary were taken to Auschwitz in summer 1944. The last deportation reached Auschwitz on 3 November 1944 and Himmler ordered the destruction of the crematoria the following day.

2.7 Conclusion

Nazi Germany's attempt to 'solve the Jewish Question' caused the following numbers of Jewish deaths: 32,000 from France and Belgium, 100,000 from the Netherlands, 60,000 from Greece, 60,000 from Yugoslavia, 140,000 from Czechoslovakia, 200,000 from Romania, 500,000 from Hungary, 2.2 mill from the Soviet Union and 2.7 mill from Poland. Also murdered were Jews from Albania, Norway, Denmark, Italy, Luxemburg and Bulgaria.[1] In the face of statistics like these, posing academic questions might seem a bit superfluous, but some do need to be addressed.

In the past, respectable German historians have argued that Hitler never ordered the Final Solution, rather he sanctioned actions being carried out by subordinates and permitted the Holocaust grow up gradually.[2] Such an interpretation is no longer credible. Given how the Third Reich worked and the nature of the speeches given by Hitler at key points during the development of the Third Reich, it is implausible that he did not effectively 'order' the Final Solution at some point. At the very least this was done through a 'nod and wink' in talks to key staff. His horrid rhetoric was designed to let people know what he wanted and the meetings gave a sense of 'everyone being in this together.' But his instigation may also have taken a more direct form. One of Hitler's secretaries recalled a secret meeting between the Führer and Himmler during spring 1941 after which the head of the SS looked so shaken that she believed Hitler had told him to implement the Final Solution.[3] Later, in August 1941 (the same day

---

tions productivity and various Nazi manufacturers complained.
1. Benz, *Der Holocaust*, p. 116. Even this is not an exhaustive list of victims.
2. See H. Mommsen, 'The Realization of the Unthinkable: The Final Solution of the Jewish Question in the Third Reich', in H. Mommsen, *From Weimar to Auschwitz* (Cambridge: Polity Press, 1991) and M. Broszat, 'Hitler and the Genesis of the Final Solution. An Assessment of David Irving's Thesis', in H.W. Koch (ed.), *Apects of the Third Reich* (London: MacMillan, 1985).
3. G. Sereny, *Albert Speer. His Battle with the Truth* (London: Picador, 1995), pp. 248–9.

he was sick at the shooting near Minsk), Himmler told Otto Bradfisch, the leader of *Einsatzkommando 8*, that Hitler personally had ordered the elimination of the Jews.[1]

It has also been suggested that the Holocaust grew out of a failing war effort and resulting administrative chaos. As Hans Mommsen puts it:

> The eventual step towards mass destruction occurred at the end of a complex political process. During this process, internal antagonisms within the system gradually blocked all alternative options, so that the physical liquidation of the Jews ultimately appeared to be the only way out.[2]

Administration in the Third Reich was indeed chaotic and this did impact on the treatment of Jews and the conduct of resettlement projects. Likewise the failed war effort prevented Jewish resettlement to both Madagascar and Siberia. Obviously there were resulting pressures, but these should not be turned into the actual cause of the murder of six million people. Chaos and a lost war provided the circumstances under which the Final Solution was chosen, but the choice itself can only be explained by decisive reference to the basic hatred which put mass murder on the agenda in the first place.

A more interesting point to think about is when the Holocaust actually began. Did it really only start in March 1942 when gas chambers and death camps began to operate in earnest? This implies that the *Einsatzgruppen* were not part of a dedicated plan to exterminate all the Jews of Europe. As Mommsen puts it, they 'led to' but were 'not identical with, the subsequent Final Solution.'[3] Of course this raises the issue 'what exactly was the Holocaust?' If you take it to mean only the fully industrialised pursuit of complete physical annihilation, then it is true that the event did not start until spring 1942. If, however, you interpret the word as meaning the destruction of the Jewish 'nation' in Europe, then that aim certainly did include the actions of the *Einsatzgruppen* from the moment they entered the occupied East in June 1941. It was also expressed in various earlier resettlement plans. Admittedly there was still a transition from a policy that accepted extensive numbers of deaths as a by-product of other kinds of action (such as resettlement, slave labour or security 'cleansing') to a policy that involved complete killing for its own sake. But if you believe that from an early time events were being driven by a consistent and atrocious will to destroy as many of Europe's Jews and their communities as practically possible, then the difference between the two positions is not actually so great.

---

1   Aly, *Final Solution*, p. 22.
2   Mommsen, 'Realization of the Unthinkable', p. 240.
3   Ibid, p. 235.

The overall impression has to be that the events culminating in 'Auschwitz' owed a lot to hardening attitudes in spring 1941 and their fresh expression in July of the same year. These developments, of course, took strength from the basic idea of anti-Semitism. As chapter 1 showed, Hitler's brand of the prejudice had long contained really radical possibilities. Indeed even though Himmler's memorandum of May 1940 dismissed direct killing, it seems that in marginal notes made in his copy of *Mein Kampf* in 1927 he talked about holding 'Hebrew corruptors' under gas.[1]

From the start of the Second World War, there was a series of gradual steps which led to the transformation of such basic ideas into a practical programme. The steps moved as follows: from extensive death through resettlement to extermination through labour in the East, from the shooting of many to the shooting of most, and finally to the gassing of all. In this way the Holocaust was a dramatic part of Hitler's plan to alter the whole demography of Central and Eastern Europe to the advantage of Germany. But the severity of the motivation and uniqueness of the actual techniques of murder applied to the Jews also define the Holocaust as unique.

---

1   Breitman, *Architect of Genocide*, p. 16.

Chapter 3 The motives of the perpetrators

3.1 Introduction

Why did individuals commit these crimes? The study of motivation has to grapple with psychological characteristics which need not have left explicit traces in the historical record. After all, there might have been issues which an actor 'just assumed' or 'took for granted.' And when written evidence exists, such as personal letters or diaries, the contents need not be objective, representative or even true. Admittedly there is the possibility of carrying out an oral history project, but it may not be possible even for an interview to re-create the immediacy and complexity of an historical situation—particularly if the event in question happened decades ago and is judged shameful today. Oral evidence gathered as part of a criminal investigation obviously is an even more difficult source of information because participants would hardly want to incriminate themselves.

By its very nature, motivation is likely to vary from person to person, from day to day—and even according to mood. More than likely, any given action reflects several different factors influencing an individual's life at any given moment. So, taking the example of a racist incident on a train, a Nazi party member abused a Jew in a way that made plain he was genuinely anti-Semitic. But the Nazi also owed money to the Jew in question.[1] In this light, what motivated the attack—anti-Semitism or financial frustration? Perhaps both played a part.

We need to relate our discussion to the first chapter of this book. Just because sometimes violent anti-Semitism historically had been a notable feature in some areas of German society, we still have to be careful about the way we link the prejudice to the implementation of the Holocaust. Even senior Nazis were not always completely in agreement about anti-Semitism. Hitler's prejudice consistently came with a dangerously hard edge that was linked to practical issues like economics and conspiracy. By contrast, Governor General Hans Frank and Reich Foreign Minister Joachim von Ribbentrop were not anti-Semites as young men and only 'grew into' the prejudice

---

1   The case is discussed in more detail in M. Housden, *Resistance and Conformity in the Third Reich* (London: Routledge, 1997), pp. 142–3.

during their careers in the party.[1] If there was so much variation in prejudice at the top of the Third Reich, then German society must have been even more varied. Different people felt anti-Semitism to different degrees and responded to Nazism's messages in different ways

It should hardly be surprising that such a difficult topic as motivation has been treated in patchy fashion in the past. When the major war criminals stood trial in Nuremberg in 1946, the tribunal focused pretty much exclusively on what defendants did and what they knew to have been happening.[2] Their motives for participating in the Third Reich were not explored in detail; they were just assumed to be typically criminal. Something similar happened at the trial of Adolf Eichmann in Jerusalem in the early 1960s. In this case, questions of motive were raised when he pleaded 'not guilty in the sense of the indictment' to charges associated with the Holocaust. Unfortunately the court did not explore what he meant.[3] Eichmann was found guilty on the basis of participation itself, but his motives were left to an academic to discuss after his execution. This gap in the treatment of motive on the part of the law courts matters because such important events have helped colour how the Nazis have been perceived by the wider world.[4]

Motive also matters because it is a substantial intellectual challenge to understand evil—particularly when practiced by well educated people in a cultured nation. Grappling with this problem has led to a great deal of important scholarly work. In psychology, Stanley Milgram's famous experiments about obedience were motivated by trying to understand participation in the Third Reich.[5] Philosopher Hannah Arendt analysed Eichmann and developed the idea of 'the banality of evil' (see below).[6] Sociologist Zygmunt Baumann has discussed the way life in large organisations helps generate the conditions for inhuman behaviour (see below).[7] And academics are not the only people interested here. Relatives of victims and perpetrators alike

---

1   M. Bloch, *Ribbentrop* (London: Bantam Press, 1992), p. 206.
2   See M. Housden, *Hans Frank. Lebensraum and the Holocaust* (Basingstoke: Palgrave, 2003), chapter 11.
3   H. Arendt, *Eichmann in Jerusalem. A Report on the Banality of Evil* (London: Penguin, 1994), p. 25.
4   Ibid, p. 221.
5   See K. Deaux and L. S. Wrightsman, *Social Psychology* (Belmont, CA.: Wadsworth, 1988), chapter 8. In an experiment Milgram found that an alarming number of people were willing to give a lethal electric shock to another person if ordered to do so by an authority figure. Interestingly, those who refused included individuals of German background who seemed to have learned an important lesson from their country's history.
6   Arendt, *Eichmann in Jerusalem*, p. 252.
7   Z. Baumann, *Modernity and the Holocaust* (Oxford: Polity Press, 1989).

have shown a clear 'need' to understand the carnage that happened during the Second World War. In the mid-1990s, this 'need' provided the basis for the massive popular success of Daniel Goldhagen's book *Hitler's Willing Executioners*. We will start our discussion of historical literature with this text.

3.2 *Hitler's Willing Executioners*, Daniel Goldhagen

Goldhagen's book caused such a stir that it was followed by a collection of letters written to the author by ordinary readers. Lots of the responses were positive, for instance saying that it was most important for Germany that he had written it.[1] So what had he said? Goldhagen's argument was very simple: popular violent anti-Semitic beliefs caused the participation of ordinary Germans in the Holocaust. To use his words:

> Not economic hardship, not the coercive means of a totalitarian state, not social psychological pressure, not invariable psychological propensities, but ideas about Jews that were pervasive in Germany, and had been for decades, induced ordinary Germans to kill unarmed, defenceless Jewish men, women and children by the thousands, systematically and without pity.[2]

Goldhagen focused on German reserve police men who had executed Jews in the East between 1941 and 1945. He said that since almost a quarter of a million men had been involved, they must have been typical of German society as a whole and their participation was evidence of a fault line running through their national consciousness. Goldhagen proposed that culturally-determined ways of thinking dating back to the Middle Ages ensured that all Germans suffered from 'cognitive' anti-Semitism. By the mid-point of the twentieth century, German society had become infected by 'a demonological anti-Semitism, of the virulent variety' which provided the foundation for such a murderous race hatred that the 'genocidal killing of Jews' became 'a German national project.'[3] Hence he coined a phrase: 'no Germans, no Holocaust.'[4] So although Goldhagen accepted that various eastern European peoples also took part in the Holocaust, only Germans provided the drive to force events forwards.[5]

According to Goldhagen, then, the Third Reich witnessed an almost 'universally

---

1 D. J. Goldhagen (ed.), *Briefe an Goldhagen* (Berlin: Goldmann, 1998), p. 28.
2 D. J. Goldhagen, *Hitler's Willing Executioners. Ordinary Germans and the Holocaust* (London: Little, Brown and Company, 1996), p. 9.
3 Ibid, pp. 7, 11 and 392–3.
4 Ibid, p. 6.
5 Ibid, p. 6.

held' ideology that sought to 'eliminate' Jewish influence from society once and for all.[1] This alone explained why Germans did not simply kill Jews, but did so in ways that were degrading and horrible. The perpetrators of the Holocaust did not have to cut the beards of Orthodox Jews or make old men perform circus tricks. They did not have to use whips on their captives, unleash dogs on them or burn them alive in synagogues. But Germans were cruel whenever the possibility arose.[2] Likewise, no one could have compelled so very many Germans to implement the Holocaust with enthusiasm rather than reluctance. But most German perpetrators chose to be zealous and six million people died as a result.

A few academics greeted *Hitler's Willing Executioners* warmly. Colin Richmond agreed the photographs of people committing genocide gave the game away. There were 'too many smiles on the faces of killers.'[3] But Goldhagen encountered a great deal of hostility too. Writing to him, an ordinary citizen from Hamburg denounced his study as one-sided since he had never witnessed anti-Semitism in northern Germany before 1939.[4] By far the majority of academics queued up to follow this more critical line. Steven Aschheim accused the book of dealing in national stereotypes and popularist interpretations of the past.[5] Geoff Eley said that Goldhagen, without good evidence, turned silence on the part of most Germans when faced with persecution into support for violent anti-Semitism.[6] Hans-Ulrich Wehler accused Goldhagen of 'demonising' Germans without including an adequate comparative angle addressing anti-Semitism as it was displayed by other nationalities.[7] Istvan Deak added to the point by observing that hundreds of thousands of Estonians, Lithuanians, Latvians, Ukrainians and Romanians had been perpetrators too.[8] Under the circumstances it was not legitimate to denounce Germans as anti-Semites but ignore these other groups more or less completely. The lack of a comparative perspective was pursued further by Ruth Birn who pointed out that Goldhagen did not locate the genocide of

---

1   Ibid, p. 48.
2   Ibid, p. 377.
3   C. Richmond, 'Acceptable Atrocity', in *Immigrants and Minorities* 15 (1996) p. 277
4   Goldhagen (ed.), *Briefe an Goldhagen*, p. 112.
5   S. E. Aschheim, 'Archetypes and the German–Jewish Dialogue: Reflections Occasioned by the Goldhagen Affair', in *German History* 15 (1997) pp. 240–2.
6   G. Eley, 'Ordinary Germans, Nazis, and Judeocide' in G. Eley (ed.), *The Goldhagen Effect. History, Memory, Nazism—Facing the German Past* (Ann Arbor: University of Michigan Press, 2000), p. 11.
7   H-U. Wehler, 'The Goldhagen Controversy: Agonizing Problems, Scholarly Failure and the Political Dimension , in *German History* 15 (1997) pp. 84–7.
8   I. Deak, 'Holocaust Views: The Goldhagen Controversy in Retrospect', in *Central European History* 30 (1997) pp. 301

the Jews in the wider context of occupation policies.¹ After all, atrocities were not just committed against Jews, so what significance should we give this fact? Birn also argued that *Hitler's Willing Executioners* presented its source evidence in ways that were biased and selective. Specifically she said that the interviews with policemen used by Goldhagen also contained expressions of shame and disgust at their actions, but Goldhagen did not take these comments seriously.

Norman Finkelstein has been Daniel Goldhagen's fiercest critic. He has said:

> Replete with gross misrepresentations of source material and internal contradictions, *Hitler's Willing Executioners* is devoid of scholarly value.

He maintains that, even during the war years, most Germans were repelled by the very idea of violent anti-Semitism and that, correspondingly, the history of the prejudice in Germany was more complicated than Goldhagen implies. In the process Finkelstein raises some interesting questions, not least this one: how should we evaluate the fact that 3,000 black Americans were lynched in the USA between 1890 and 1930, but such a treatment of Jews was inconceivable even in pre-war Nazi Germany?²

All in all, despite its commercial success, there was extensive agreement that something was not quite right about Goldhagen's work. Admittedly a number of arguments similar to his had been made decades earlier without arousing quite such an outcry. A long tradition of historians had tried to explain Nazism in terms of German intellectual developments since the time of Luther.³ Also, in his classic text, Raul Hilberg noted that Germany's 'machinery of destruction' had been so massive that its staff must have been typical of German society as a whole.⁴ But Goldhagen had been too unsubtle in his treatment of anti-Semitism. Even if we realise well that anti-Semitism was not uncommon in Weimar Germany,⁵ an adequate account of how its importance grew so massively needs to take a closer look at the lives of specific individuals. Hence even Gitta Sereny's biographical study of Franz Stangl, commandant of Treblinka and Sobibór, does not reduce his life to anti-Semitism alone.⁶ Rather she finds that, regardless of his original feelings about Jews, he became a participant in

---

1 R. B. Birn, 'Revising the Holocaust', in *Historical Journal* 40 (1997) pp. 195–215.
2 Finkelstein and Birn, *A Nation on Trial*, p. 50.
3 For instance W. M. McGovern, *From Luther to Hitler* (New York: Houghton Mifflin, 1973).
4 R. Hilberg, *The Destruction of the European Jews* (New York: New Viewpoints, 1973), p. 643.
5 U. Herbert, 'Vernichtungspolitik. Neue Antworten und Fragen zur Geschichte des "Holocaust"', in U. Herbert (ed), *Nationalsozialistische Vernichtungspolitik 1939–1945* (Frankfurt aM: Fischer, 1998), p. 42.
6 G. Sereny, 'Colloquy with a Conscience', in *The German Trauma. Experiences and Reflections 1938–2000* (London: Penguin, 2000) and *Into that Darkness* (New York: Vintage, 1983).

the killing process only through a series of incremental steps each of which he found hard to reject at the time. He became a killer through a gradual process of personal corruption, not simply because of belief in a horrid prejudice pure and simple.

3.3 *Ordinary Men,* **Christopher Browning**

Christopher Browning has tried to provide a more nuanced treatment of those committing Hitler's crimes. He studied the same men as Daniel Goldhagen, namely the members of Reserve Police Battalion 101.[1] His work gives a gritty portrayal of how they secured Łódź ghetto in 1940, guarded trainloads of Jews deported from Germany, Austria and the Protectorate during 1941 and spring 1942, before becoming a front line force perpetrating genocide in summer 1942. Browning's work relies on the same sources as Goldhagen (i.e. investigation materials compiled by the state prosecutor of Hamburg between 1962 and 1972), but interprets them very differently.

In July 1942 the unit drew up at the Polish village of Jósefów. The men were told by their officer what they were about to do and were given the chance not to participate. About a dozen of the 500 fell out, while the rest spent the day shooting all the members of the village's Jewish community. Browning's book makes plain it was a gruesome affair indeed but goes on to show how Battalion 101 learned from the horrors of that day. Next time they had to shoot a large number of Jews, they used former concentration camp inmates to do the killing. In upshot, by November 1942, Battalion 101 had killed 6,500 Polish Jews—and the statistics would only rise. In autumn 1943, Senior SS leader Odilo Globocnik decided to liquidate all the Jews still working in camps in his corner of the Government General. 101 participated in 'Action Harvest Festival' and shot 30,500 people in only a couple of days.

The facts alone make us wonder what sort of people would do such things. Now we come to the significance of the book's title. Browning believes the men of Battalion 101 were so 'ordinary' that anyone, if placed in the same position, would have participated alongside them. In his words, if 'the men of Reserve Police Battalion 101 could become killers under such circumstances, what group of men cannot?'[2] On the face of it, rank and file members of the group were indeed 'ordinary.' Mostly drawn from the lower middle and working classes, aged between 37 and 42 and with only 25% of their number party members in 1942, we might have expected more to have

---

[1] C. Browning, *Ordinary Men: Reserve Police Battalion 101 and the Final Solution in Poland* (New York: Harper Collins, 1993).

[2] Browning, *Ordinary Men*, p. 189.

refused to shoot helpless civilians. In the event, however, 80% of the shooters completed their dreadful task even on the first day in Józefów.

The reasons for their behaviour become all the more enigmatic when we know that reprisals against people who refused to shoot Jews were forbidden, they could be relieved of their duties at any time and the official political indoctrination process applied in the battalion was weak. Browning also found in the interrogations that 'the whole question of anti-Semitism is marked by silence.'[1] He implies that it had not been a major motivating factor for the policemen. Relatedly Browning notes stories suggesting the men had refused to kill Jews whom they knew (e.g. their kitchen staff).

Rather than race hatred and ideology, Browning suggests the men of 101 were motivated by a number of 'ordinary' factors. They experienced 'peer pressure.' A long way from home, they needed the support of their colleagues just to get from day to day and would not risk becoming outcasts by refusing to shoot Jews. Drawing on psychological experiments, Browning notes how Stanley Milgram showed that most people are naturally inclined to 'follow orders.' Likewise the experiments of Philip Zimbardo are deployed to show that we tend to conform to whatever role we are allocated in society.[2] Putting everything together, Browning maintains that all of these normal pressures, supplemented by the fact that almost daily killing 'habituated' the men into atrocity and that the experience of war encouraged them to think in terms of 'friends and foe' (which in their world became 'Aryans and Jews'), explain participation in the Holocaust.

But has Browning gone too far in his rejection of racism? It is fair to suppose that when interviewed by prosecutors in the 1960s, the former members of 101 were reluctant to express anti-Semitic convictions, so their evidence might be tainted in this respect. Also we want to know why so many of the men carried out the massacres at Józefów when they were not yet habituated into murder and were told they could fall out. Peer pressure alone is unlikely to have been a strong enough force to have determined this decision. In a later book Browning does, however, provide an interesting case study of clearing a ghetto at Marcinkance. Here he makes clear that while some men refused to participate at all, and others refused at certain points to shoot fleeing Jews, there was a 'hard core' of dedicated anti-Semites who killed with

---

1   Ibid, p. 73.
2   In his experiment at Stanford University, Zimbardo set up an experimental prison and divided a group of students into prisoners and jailers. Over the experimental period he observed how students in the different groups began to conform the roles they were given. Zimbardo had to stop the experiment early because some guards began behaving in too brutally.

enthusiasm (i.e. 4 out of 17 participants).¹ In other words, it is likely that participants always exhibited different levels of enthusiasm for anti-Semitic actions. No doubt they had different reasons for participation too, ranging from largely ideological to predominantly 'normal.' If this point is rather obvious, let's start to explore motivation and the Holocaust from a different angle.

3.4 Bureaucracy and genocide

The participation of hundreds of thousands of people in a project to kill millions meant that the whole affair had to be managed and administered. Hitler's early comments that 'emotional' anti-Semitism only produced pogroms while 'rational' anti-Semitism would be more thorough showed that he was aware of the benefits of getting things properly organised.² It was also clear that once whole organisations were set up to deal with the Jewish Question, they would keep pushing the issue forward. In other words, the Holocaust was not just industrialised genocide, it was bureaucratic genocide too.

Bureaucracy thrives on things being done in an orderly, well-regulated manner, and an orderly kind of racism was more acceptable to the German public. The German population never liked unexpected outbursts of violence in the streets where they lived. The bureaucratic organisation of events also raised the possibility that a great many officials could participate in events (for instance making sure that deportation trains ran on time) as if they were doing any other kind of job.³ So given the importance of bureaucracy and bureaucrats in the Holocaust, there are a great many issues to explore about how the project was conducted. For instance, Raul Hilberg observed that (notwithstanding what we have said already) German bureaucracy persecuted the Jews with so much greater efficiency than the bureaucracies of Germany's allies, that we must wonder how German bureaucrats dealt with their moral scruples from day to day. He also wondered why the more enlightened values typical of life in Weimar Germany did not upset the administration of the Holocaust.⁴

There have been a number of famous texts relating to bureaucrats of genocide. Rudolf Höss was commandant at Auschwitz and while on trial after the war wrote his

---

1   C. R. Browning, *Nazi Policy, Jewish Workers, German Killers* (CUP, 2000), p. 166.
2   C. R. Browning, 'The German Bureaucracy and the Holocaust', in A. Grobman and D. Landes (eds.), *Critical Issues of the Holocaust* (Dallas, Texas: Rossel Books, 1983), pp. 145–8.
3   Ibid.
4   R. Hilberg, *The Destruction of the European Jews* (New York: New Viewpoints, 1973), p. 646.

memoirs.¹ Actually they show remarkably few signs suggesting that an unconventional man had helped bring about distinctly unconventional events. Hannah Arendt analysed Adolf Eichmann while he was on trial in Jerusalem.² Eventually hanged on 31 April 1962, a specially convened court found this former official of the Reich Security Head Office guilty of a string of charges associated with the attempted destruction of the Jews. But based on Eichmann's self-presentation in the court, Arendt began to feel that his life spoke of more than just personal mistakes. In a modern world becoming increasingly bureaucratic, she felt that Eichmann's career as a manager of genocide reflected more general issues.

Although Eichmann had organised the deportation of whole communities to Nisko and to extermination camps, Arendt still interpreted his character as 'run of the mill.' She said:

> The trouble with Eichmann was precisely that so many [bureaucrats of genocide] were like him, and that many were neither perverted nor sadistic, that they were, and still are, terribly and terrifyingly normal.³

His relations with his family were said to be better than just 'normal' and his personal motivation for participation in the Holocaust was 'an extraordinary diligence in looking out for his personal advancement.' Otherwise, when Eichmann organised genocide, he did not really understand what he was doing.⁴ On a number of occasions as Arendt explored how this could have been possible, she likened him to a machine. He was one of the 'mere cogs in the administrative machinery' of that time and place.⁵ Apparently suggesting that Eichmann had no responsibility for creating the administrative machinery in the first place, no role in deciding how it should be applied and little control over how it worked, Arendt proposed that 'sheer thoughtlessness' led him to become 'one of the greatest criminals of that period.' This thoughtlessness produced 'more havoc than all the evil instincts taken together.'⁶

This is the basis on which Arendt judged Eichmann 'ordinary.' Inhabiting an institution dedicated to the task of genocide, he went about his daily and largely desk-bound routine failing to comprehend the full consequences of his actions. He just

---

1   R. Höss, *Commandant at Auschwitz* (London: Phoenix Press, 2000).
2   Arendt, *Eichmann in Jerusalem*. For a more recent study of Eichmann, see D. Cesarani, *Eichmann. His Life and Crimes* (London: Heinemann, 2004).
3   Ibid, p. 276.
4   Ibid, p. 287.
5   Ibid, p. 153 and 289.
6   Ibid, p. 288.

could not stand back and glimpse the bigger picture. Arendt thought this was a dreadfully 'normal' response to working in a large, modern institution and she proposed that 'every bureaucracy' could 'dehumanize' its staff in a comparable way.[1] She said this situation epitomised 'the banality of evil.'[2] Her interpretation captured the imagination of many later academics.

3.5 Bureaucracy and the modern world

Zygmunt Baumann took Arendt's arguments a stage further. For him, the way a bureaucracy works contains 'all the technical elements' required to permit genocide.[3] For instance, a large organisation works best when its members of staff have few personal ethical standards, but remain sufficiently malleable to be 'good, efficient and diligent' workers no matter what they are asked to do.[4] Hence institutions marginalise individuals who might cause problems on account of personal principles. Baumann also believes bureaucracies generate perpetual pressures to find the most efficient (as opposed to the most humane) solution to any given problem. Putting these points together can turn a bureaucracy into a 'loaded dice.' Once such an organisation is set up to deal with an issue, certainly it keeps pursuing this mission in order to justify its existence. In addition, however, because large organisations emphasise values such as cost-effectiveness rather than fellow-feeling, there is always a likelihood they will discover unpalatable ways to deal with the tasks for which they are responsible.[5]

The management hierarchy typical of a bureaucracy makes it easier to do bad things. Orders trickle down from the 'top' of an organisation to the 'bottom' and on the way seem to acquire an authoritative force, even the quality of a moral obligation, as a 'superior' administrator tells a 'junior' what to do. This attribute becomes exaggerated when the organisation designates some people 'experts' who seem to possess far more knowledge about a topic than their colleagues and members of the public. In fact, the experience of being a single link in the whole bureaucratic system leading from key policy decisions taken at the 'top' to their implementation at the 'bottom', encourages an individual to feel a lack of personal responsibility for what is happening. A senior member of a bureaucracy finds it easy to take a nasty decision because, safe in an office far removed from its consequences, he will not have to grapple with

---

1   Ibid, p. 288.
2   Ibid, p. 252.
3   Z. Baumann, *Modernity and the Holocaust* (Oxford: Polity Press, 1989), p. 104.
4   Ibid, p. 102.
5   Ibid, p. 104.

its implementation. Mid-level officials interpret themselves as simply intermediaries who are only passing things 'down the line,' while those actually implementing policy 'at the coal face' inevitably are junior staff with the whole weight of an organisation bearing down on them. How can the latter refuse any demand?

All these characteristics plausibly help bureaucracies produce actions which individuals might not carry out if left to their own devices, and Baumann's analysis meshes well with Hans Mommsen's reading of the Holocaust. He thinks that the creation of mass, impersonal and technical ways of killing (such as the gas chamber) helped people suppress possible qualms about what they were doing.[1] It was also important that bureaucrats could rationalise their behaviour as actually in the victim's best interests. Mommsen argues that as the position of the Jews in ghettos in the East deteriorated during winter 1941–42, then German officials could tell themselves it would actually be more humane to kill them quickly rather than wait for a slow death from cold, starvation or disease.[2]

3.3 Criticisms of bureaucratic theory

Unfortunately the views of Arendt and Baumann do not give us the full story. As David Cesarani's recent biography of Eichmann makes clear, although as a young man he was not a radical anti-Semite, at some stage Eichmann had to *choose* to become a perpetrator of genocide.[3] Could this choice really have been 'banal' and could Eichmann actually have turned himself into a 'cog in a machine' as a result? Indeed, could the demands of bureaucratic life really have overpowered all the other characteristics of what it is to be human?

Michael Thad Allen's study of mid-level SS camp managers tells us these were not well trained bureaucrats.[4] They were less educated party men in search of a job. Their efforts at administration were sloppy and, far from being 'cogs in a machine' they thought of themselves as 'big fish' in their particular 'small pond' who could wield authority. They did not sit back and wait for orders from a superior, but knew they had a lot of autonomy when it came to running their particular facilities. What's more Allen found their paperwork crammed full of Nazi ideology. These men seemed passionately involved in what they were doing.

---

1 Mommsen, 'Realization of the Unthinkable', p. 250.
2 See Höppner's memorandum in chapter 1.
3 Cesarani, *Eichmann*.
4 M. T. Allen, 'The Banality of Evil Reconsidered: SS Mid-Level Managers of Extermination Through Work', in *Central European History* 30 (1997) pp. 253–94.

We must question whether Nazi bureaucrats ever really could have been disinterested administrators. On the one hand, the Hitler State was such a chaotic place that people had to enter into events whole-heartedly or else face insignificance. What's more, senior officials generally tried hard to promote an anti-Semitic spirit in the workforce. This was why, when he spoke to his juniors, Governor General Hans Frank sometimes referred to Jews as lice, vermin and parasites. He even made bad jokes about their suffering which, incidentally, seem to have been greeted by shouts of 'Bravo!' from the audience.[1] So there is much to be said in favour of M.R.Marrus's comment:

> In the final analysis the destruction of the Jews was not so much a product of laws and commands as it was a matter of spirit, of shared comprehension, of consonance and synchronization.[2]

A comparative perspective suggests that specifically German organisations were uniquely culpable in committing genocide during the Second World War. Long ago Raul Hilberg pointed out that Nazi officials in the East were few in number and overstretched in their jobs. But he also observed:

> The German administration, however, was not deterred by the pressures of other assignments; it never resorted to pretences [not to implement anti-Semitic policies], like the Italians, it never took token measures, like the Hungarians, it never procrastinated, like the Bulgarians. The German bureaucrats worked efficiently, in haste, and with a sense of urgency. Unlike their collaborators, the Germans never did the minimum. They always did the maximum.[3]

Jonathan Steinberg's comparison of the German and Italian armies reaches a similarly unfortunate conclusion. To his knowledge, every single Jew who fell into the hands of the *Wehrmacht* went to a concentration camp, but not a single one under the authority of the Italian army suffered that fate. Steinberg concluded that, when it came to dealing with Jews, the two armies 'inhabited different moral universes.'[4]

---

1   Hans Frank's official diary. Federal Archive, Berlin. Entry of 18 May 1940. R52 II / 177.
2   M. R. Marrus, *The Holocaust in History* (London: Penguin, 1993), p. 49.
3   Hilberg, *Destruction of European Jewry*, p. 644.
4   J. Steinberg, *All or Nothing: The Axis and the Holocaust 1941–43* (London: Routledge, 1990), p. 219.

3.4 Conclusion

What motivated ordinary Germans to participate in the Holocaust? A convincing answer requires a careful balancing act. Germany certainly had a history of vicious anti-Semitism, and Nazi Party ideology fitted the trend. But Goldhagen goes too far when he turns anti-Semitism into the sole cause of popular participation in genocide. It is obviously that the events of 1941 to 1945 could not have happened in 1933, not even in 1939. So it is indeed plausible that some process of change happened in Germany that turned genocide into a practical possibility. Over the years, popular attitudes to Jews must have been corroded, first thanks to Nazi rule and then the experience of war. Likewise we can believe that some people (perhaps like Stangl[1]) were drawn into genocide gradually, in a manner that made it hard to draw a line at any given point. It is also possible that both the men of Reserve Police Battalion 101 and the office bureaucrats involved in the Holocaust did have a number of things on their minds during the war years, with anti-Semitism being just one of them. But our analysis must not stop at this point.

Not all Germans ever became enthusiastic anti-Semites, but as Browning's case study of ghetto clearing in Marcinkance shows, some were. Perhaps their certainty helped pull along the doubters with whom they rubbed shoulders on a daily basis. As Raul Hilberg says, time and again the perpetrators of the Holocaust had to confront what they were doing and overcome the sort of moral scruples which must have been the order of the day during the Weimar years.[2] In the end, this can only have been possible if most found a way to convince themselves that what they were doing was right. Such a step might only have come with actual participation. That is to say, people might only have adopted anti-Semitism as a means to justifying involvement in a dreadful initiative which previously they would never have thought possible. But when faced with the Holocaust, we really should accept quite firmly that racism cannot be air-brushed out of the picture. Although the exact relationship between anti-Semitism and participation in the Holocaust has not been defined once and for all, it has to remain the single most important component of a convincing explanation.

---

1 See chapter 2.
2 Hilberg, *Destruction of the European Jews*, p. 649.

Chapter 4 How bystanders reacted

4.1 Introduction

What is a 'bystander'? Neither the perpetrator of the action in question nor its object, a 'bystander' is someone who witnesses events occurring between others without intervening directly. In the context of the Holocaust, therefore, calling someone a 'bystander' sounds like criticism. How could anyone have observed what was happening and not tried to intervene to stop it? True, quite a few people who began as bystanders did eventually become 'resisters' to Nazism. No small number of Jewish lives were saved as a result. But the sad fact remains that the majority of people were more passive than this. So if today we flatter ourselves with the hope that we would have tried to do something to help Hitler's victims, why did so many Europeans stay out of the Jewish Question between 1939 and 1945? Were they afraid of the personal consequences of intervention? Were they indifferent about the fate of strangers? Or could they have had some sympathy for the removal of Jews from society?

Issues of blame are unavoidable when we talk about bystanders. In the background stands a suggestion that a moral duty was evaded. Should the German population as a whole (indeed other national populations in Central and Eastern Europe too) be blamed for permitting such horrible events to happen under their noses? Should we apply an idea of 'collective guilt' to populations of whole regions for letting fellow human beings down badly? And how far should blame stretch? Could Allied statesmen have done more to disrupt the Holocaust? Could Jewish communities in Britain and the USA have done more to assist their co-religionists in peril? And did Christian spiritual leaders (most notably the Pope) respond adequately to the demands of the time? If Pius XII was largely silent, why was this? Was his silence designed to give priests 'space' to save Jewish lives in secret, or did it indicate indifference? When we talk about 'bystanders,' we have to address some extremely tough questions.

4.2 Germans as bystanders

How much did average Germans know about the genocide being carried out in their name? Although mass killing was supposed to happen under conditions of secrecy and at locations well removed from the German heartland, many Germans had a shrewd idea of what was going on. American intelligence units gained this impression as they entered Germany towards the end of the war.[1] It was hard for people to avoid putting two and two together. Not only had they observed Jews being deported from their own communities, but as the war went badly (particularly in 1942) they heard Hitler and Goebbels say the most inflammatory things. So when, in early 1943, German propaganda broadcasted the discovery at Katyn (near Smolensk) of the bodies of thousands of Polish army officers who clearly had been shot by the Soviet secret police (NKVD), the popular response was 'that's just what we've done to the Jews.'[2]

Sometimes knowledge of events was remarkably apposite. There was a rumour in Germany that Jews were being gassed in a railway tunnel—albeit at a site not far from Berlin.[3] Actually some knowledge was just about inevitable. The BBC broadcast to Germany about atrocities in the East and soldiers returning from the front brought stories back with them. So Germans lived with the knowledge that very bad things indeed were happening, perhaps alleviating their guilt by rationalising that they were 'just' excesses carried out by individual officers or Himmler rather than state sponsored genocide.[4]

During the war years, many Germans regarded the Jewish Question as a low priority issue. This is why M.R.Marrus has argued that the road to Auschwitz was built as much on indifference as anti-Semitism.[5] So although very many Germans didn't like being confronted by the brutal treatment of Jews, after 1941 especially they had other things on their minds. As one lady put it, 'Why should I care about the Jews? The only thing I care about is my brother in Russia.'[6] What's more, as it became clear Germany could not win the conflict, people had good reason to put distance between themselves and such dreadful events.

Factors like these were reinforced by the reality that in the Third Reich it was

---

[1] D. Bankier, 'German Public Awareness of the Final Solution', in D. Cesarani (ed.), *The Final Solution. Origins and Implementation* (London: Routledge, 1994), p. 216.
[2] Ibid p. 220.
[3] D. Bankier, *The Germans and the Final Solution* (Oxford: Blackwell, 1992), pp. 111–2.
[4] H. Mommsen, 'What did the Germans know about the Genocide of the Jews?', in W. H. Pehle (ed.), *November 1938* (Oxford: Berg, 1991), pp. 196–200.
[5] M. R. Marrus, *The Holocaust in History* (London: Penguin, 1993), p. 91. The assessment chimes with Ian Kershaw s work, see 'Antisemitismus und Volksmeinung. Reaktionen auf die Judenverfolgung', in M. Broszat and E. Fröhlich (eds.), *Bayern in der NS Zeit* (Munich: Oldenbourg, 1979).
[6] Bankier, *The Germans and the Final Solution*, p. 136.

never easy for people to get together to discuss publicly and critically exactly what was going on around them. This contributed to a sense of helplessness in the face of a whole state system locked in a massive war and perpetrating crimes at inaccessible sites. So although Germans were prepared to assist Jews during the early years of the Reich, with time this inclination fell away.[1] In fact, even before 1939 contacts between Jew and Gentile had become superficial. Consequently although some Germans were affronted by the introduction of the Yellow Star on German soil in autumn 1941, soon this response gave way to apathy.[2] Before long people became concerned about being labelled a '*Judenfreund*' (friend of Jews) and attracting the unwelcome attention of local Gestapo officers.[3]

There were good reasons to worry on this score, as Robert Gellately's work about policing racial policy shows only too well.[4] Too many people were not just silent on the Jewish Question, but engaged actively with the regime's demands. Gellately's information about the Gestapo in Düsseldorf and Würzburg makes clear that the direct observations of police officers and paid informers only precipitated about 5% of the total number of investigations into friendship between 'Aryans' and 'Jews.' Reports from the general population, however, led to about 57% of investigations. Admittedly average Germans denounced each other for a whole host of reasons (i.e. not just because of anti-Semitism), but even their mixed motives helped make Hitler's system 'work.'

Naturally this generalisation has to be qualified because we must also recognise that a number of Germans did take notable steps to resist Jewish policy. Between ten and twelve thousand Germans Jews tried to avoid deportation to the East, for instance by going into hiding, and in the end about 1,400 Jews survived the war in Berlin alone.[5] This was only possible because a number of 'Aryans' helped them. The German capital also witnessed an important popular demonstration against the deportation of German Jews. In February 1943, Nazi authorities were attempting to round up the

---

1   T. Maurer, 'Customers, Patients, Neighbours and Friends. Relations between Jews and non-Jews in Germany, 1933–1938', in D. Bankier and I. Gutman (eds.), *Nazi Europe and the Final Solution* (Jerusalem: Yad Vashem, 2003).
2   M. Housden, *Resistance and Conformity in the Third Reich* (London: Routledge, 1997), p. 140.
3   Mommsen, 'What did the Germans know about the Genocide of the Jews?', p. 211.
4   R. Gellately, *The Gestapo and German Society: Enforcing Racial Policy 1933–1945* (Oxford: Clarendon, 1991) and 'A Monstrous Uneasiness: Citizen Participation and Persecution of the Jews in Nazi Germany', in P. Hayes (ed.), *Lessons and Legacies: The Meaning of the Holocaust in a Changing World* (Evanston, Illinois: Northwestern University Press, 1991).
5   K. Kwiet, 'To Leave or not to Leave? The German Jews at the Crossroads', in Pehle (ed.), *November 1938*, p. 150.

last Jews in the city. Of these, about 1,800 were married to 'Aryan' women. The men were interned in the buildings of a Jewish welfare organisation on the *Rosenstrasse* and what happened next was a remarkable page in the history of the Third Reich. Up to 6,000 friends and relatives protested outside the building, day after day, and caused so much commotion that the *Gauleiter* of Berlin, Josef Goebbels, released the prisoners along with 25 others who had already been sent to Auschwitz.[1] The case showed what popular action could accomplish even in a dictatorship.

Some German churchmen also spoke out against anti-Semitism. The Protestant members of the Confessing Church issued the Barmen declaration in May 1934 rejecting Nazi ideology. We must also mention Father Lichtenberg, a Catholic priest who led his Berlin congregation openly in prayer for persecuted Jews. As a result he was imprisoned in October 1941. He was released two years later only to be interned in a labour camp where he died awaiting transportation to Dachau in November 1943.[2]

4.3 Other states: collaboration

It would, however, be wrong to focus solely on the relationship of Germans to the Holocaust. After all, Jews were not killed within the border of Germany as it had existed in the 1920s, but in the occupied lands further to the East which were populated by, among others, Poles, Ukrainians, Belorussians and the peoples of the Baltic States. Equally we must remember that large numbers of Jews were deported to death camps from occupied Western Europe, for instance from France, Belgium, Holland and Norway. Consequently we need to ask after the relationship between non-Germans and the Holocaust.

Many of the questions that arise here are still in the process of being answered, but nonetheless already some interesting studies have been published. A number of years ago, M. R. Marrus observed that collaborationist populations provided manpower which was essential to enabling the Holocaust to occur.[3] Martin Dean's study of conditions in Ukraine shows how true the point is.[4] He maintains that 25,000 Ukrainians volunteered to serve in auxiliary police units which became deeply impli-

---

1 The story is told in N. Stoltzfus, *Resistance of the Heart: Intermarriage and the Rosenstrasse Protest in Nazi Germany* (New York: Rutgers University Press, 2001).
2 For Lichtenberg's story, see K. P. Spicer, *Resisting the Third Reich: the Catholic Clergy in Hitler's Berlin* (DeKalb, Illinois: North Illinois University Press, 2004), chapter 7.
3 Marrus, *The Holocaust in History*, p. 56.
4 M. Dean, *Collaboration in the Holocaust: Crimes of the Local Police in Belorussia and Ukraine, 1941–44* (Basingstoke: Macmillan, 2000).

cated in the Holocaust. The men did not volunteer just because of anti-Semitism, there were other motives in play such as greed, ambition, alcoholism, anti-Communism, careerism and peer pressure, but the outcome was much the same. In October and November 1941 they supported *Einsatzgruppen* actions, but by 1942 in rural areas local Ukrainian police outnumbered their German counterparts by five or ten to one. Without their extensive assistance it would have been impossible to round up Jews in the countryside. Dean concludes that Jews in Ukraine often were persecuted by people who had been their neighbours and it was not just Germans who became 'willing executioners.'[1]

Nor was it only local police units that participated in the Holocaust. Joachim Tauber's work shows that Lithuania experienced a much wider kind of collaboration.[2] Certainly there were Lithuanian criminals who carried out a pogrom in Kaunas in June 1941 after being released from prison by the *Einsatzgruppen*, and a few Lithuanians staffed dedicated killing units which operated both inside their country and beyond. But, sadly, collaboration was more extensive than that. Local people became 'partisans' guarding Jews at camps set up in the woods before German authorities took them away. Local administrators liaised with Germans to circulate anti-Semitic regulations. Committees were established to organise the distribution of Jewish property once the owners had been removed. This extensive collaboration ensured that the majority of Lithuanian Jews were killed within six months of the German invasion.

It is worth pointing out that the motive for this intense persecution is particularly contentious. Tauber suggests that participation in Nazism's project must be understood in the context of the highly charged emotions which surrounded the withdrawal of Soviet forces from Lithuanian soil and the arrival of Nazi counterparts.[3] Lithuanians may well have viewed collaboration as a means to persuading Germans that their country deserved substantial independence in Hitler's Europe. Whatever the precise complex of motives in play in this part of the Baltic region, the outcome was intense.

We should not ignore what happened in other parts of Eastern Europe either. Romania, an ally of Nazi Germany, saw pogroms accompany the launch of Operation Barbarossa.[4] Arguably the most remarkable story of all, however, has been told by Jan

---

1 Ibid, p. 167.
2 J. Tauber, '"Jews. Your history on Lithuanian soil is over!" Lithuania and the Holocaust in 1941', in *Central and Eastern European Review* 1 (2007). www.ceer.org.uk.
3 Lithuania had been occupied by the Soviet Union gradually throughout 1940. Weeks before the German invasion in Jun 1941, Soviet authorities had begun to deport Lithuanians.
4 R. Ioanid, *The Holocaust in Romania: the Destruction of Jews and Gypsies under the Antonescu*

Tomasz Gross. It concerns Jedwabne, a town inhabited by Poles and Jews in roughly equal number which was situated in the area of Poland occupied by the Soviet Union in autumn 1939. Studies have already suggested that anti-Semitism was common among Poles. They have been described as indifferent to the fate of the Jews, sometimes failing to aid individuals trying to escape Nazi clutches. Some even turned Jews over to Nazi authorities and certain death.[1] Patriotic Polish underground anti-Nazi newspapers published anti-Semitic stories.[2] But what happened in Jedwabne was different again.

This was a small town which contained a community of 1,600 Jews. German troops arrived on 23 June 1941 and almost at once 'local bandits' started a pogrom. Although a priest intervened to stop the bloodshed, on 10 July Gestapo officers visited and, after holding a meeting with community representatives, sanctioned further killing. As Gross puts it, 'After this meeting the bloodbath began.'[3] What happened next was not carried out by police units of any kind, rather the mayor organised local people to torture and kill the town's Jews. 92 men participated in the massacre of all but 7 of Jedwabne's Jews. Echoing Martin Dean, Gross concludes like this:

> what the Jews saw, to their horror and, I dare say, incomprehension, were familiar faces. Not anonymous men in uniform, cogs in a war machine, agents carrying out orders, but their own neighbours, who chose to kill and were engaged in a bloody pogrom—willing executioners.[4]

For the sake of balance, we must also admit that Western Europeans helped organise the transportation of Jews to the East. In Vichy France, Maurice Papon arrested and detained about 1,600 Jews from around Bordeaux. They were taken first to Drancy camp in Paris and then Auschwitz.[5] Thanks to local collaboration, France as a whole lost 20% of its native Jewish population. Elsewhere in Western Europe things were

---

Regime, 1940–1944 (Chicago: Ivan R. Dee, 2000), chapter 3.

1. D. L. Niewyk (ed.), *The Holocaust: Problems and Perspectives of Interpretation* (Boston: Houghton Mifflin, 1997), p. 199. Y. Arad, *Belzec, Sobibor, Treblinka. The Operation Reinhard Death Camps* (Bloomington: Indiana University Press, 1987), pp. 342–4.
2. A. Friszke, 'Attitudes towards the Jews in the Polish Underground Press, 1939–1944' and S. Krakowski, 'The Polish Underground and the Jews in the Years of the Second World War', in Bankier and Gutman (eds.), *Nazi Europe and the Final Solution*, p. 173 and p. 227.
3. J. T. Gross, *Neighbours: The Destruction of the Jewish Community in Jedwabne, Poland, 1941* (London: Random House, 2003), p. 19.
4. Ibid, p. 121.
5. R. Boyce, 'The Trial of Maurice Papon for Crimes against Humanity and the Concept of Bureaucratic Crime', in R. A. Melikan (ed.), *Domestic and International Trials, 1700–2000. The Trial in History. Volume II* (MUP, 2003).

worse still. Belgium lost 40% of its Jews and the Netherlands 75%.[1]

4.3 Other states: resistance

Even with this said, some residents of states either allied to or occupied by Nazi Germany were courageous enough to keep a lantern of humanity burning. The environment in which their assistance took place could be so hostile that effectively they were risking the lives of themselves and their families. Also persecution could be so concerted that the survival of any given Jew could depend on a chance factor such as whether his physical appearance allowed him to pass as 'Gentile,' but still there were cases of help that proved successful.

Tec has recorded how 'ordinary' Poles helped.[2] For instance, a man called Jan Rybak saved a young Jewish woman by telling a hostile crowd that she was his cousin and certainly not a Jew. A woman, whose great grandmother had been Jewish and whose stories she could still remember, helped a Jewish woman by employing her 'under cover' as a housekeeper. Tec found that people like these who helped Jews were individual thinkers; they were self-reliant individuals who responded with decency when confronted by anyone at all in need. Hence Jan Rybak also saved Russian soldiers, and even (late in the war) a German who was threatened by an angry mob. Tec says that cases like these mean that the Holocaust not only tells us about 'man's inhumanity to man,' but his 'humanity to man' as well.

In Latvia, Paul Schiemann was a well known ethnic German who had a long history of promoting liberal politics. By 1941 he was almost 70 years old and was in ill health, so rather than risk a scandal by sending him to a camp, Nazi authorities left him at home under house arrest. Here he managed to save a young Jewish girl by employing her as a servant. Later in life the former servant girl said Schiemann had been a unique individual who created an 'ethical microclimate' in his home, even in the face of Nazi occupation policies.[3] Raul Wallenberg was another notable individual who acted to save Jewish lives.[4] He was a Swedish diplomat working in Budapest in 1944. By writing out Swedish identity documents for thousands of the city's Jews

---

1 M. Marrus and R. Paxton, 'Western Europeans and the Jews', in Niewyk (ed.), *The Holocaust*, p. 249.
2 N.Tec, 'Helping Behaviour and Rescue during the Holocaust', in P. Hayes (ed.), *Lessons and Legacies. The Meaning of the Holocaust in a Changing World* (Evanston, Illinois: Northwestern University Press, 1991).
3 J. Hiden, *Defender of Minorities: Paul Schiemann, 1876–1944* (London: Hurst, 2004), p. 243.
4 Marrus, *The Holocaust in History*, p. 178.

he managed to prevent them being deported to Auschwitz.[1]

Sometimes whole communities drew together to help Jews. Chambon-sur-Mer was a small town in Vichy France which became home to over a thousand Jews who were kept safe from deportation. Two village pastors, including André Troccmé, led the villagers in this undertaking.[2] In Italy, the whole national group seemed to reject the Holocaust. Hence although the Fascist government passed racial legislation in 1938, no Jews were deported until after the fall of Mussolini at which point Germany imposed more direct control on the country.[3]

And then there was the case of Denmark. On 1 October 1943, German authorities began to round up the country's Jews. At this point the whole population spontaneously helped most of the 7,000 people flee to Sweden.[4] Consequently less than 500 Jews were taken to Theresienstadt ghetto. These developments were made possible by a mixture of factors, not least the proximity of neutral Sweden and the fact that news of the impending round up was leaked to the Danes by German authorities. Nonetheless an impression remains that in saving their fellow citizens who happened to be Jewish, Danes 'reacted spontaneously to their offended sense of democracy, humanity or basic national sentiments represented by the crime of the Final Solution.'[5]

4.4 The Vatican and the Holocaust

The last observation actually makes us want to inquire more closely about the nature of ethical leadership in Europe during these fateful years. Shouldn't we have expected more people to have reacted like the Danes, and shouldn't we have expected more community leaders to have encouraged them to do so? Religion and morality are closely linked, in principle at least. Christ's dictum 'Love your brother as yourself' had a clear moral message which was at odds with Hitler's politics. Given that the Pope is the hub of the spiritual world for Catholics, we cannot ignore questions about the Vatican's response to the Holocaust.

During the 1920s Eugenio Pacelli was Papal Nuncio in Germany and in 1933

---

1   See details about his career and the mystery of his death while in Soviet custody after the end of the war at http://www.jewishvirtuallibrary.org/jsource/biography/wallenberg.html.
2   S. Milton, 'The Righteous who helped Jews', in A. Grobman and D. Landes (eds.), *Critical Issues of the Holocaust* (Dallas, Texas: Rossell Books, 1983), p. 283.
3   See J. Steinberg, *All or Nothing: The Axis and the Holocaust 1941–43* (London: Routledge, 1990).
4   H. Kirchhoff, 'The Rescue of the Danish Jews in October 1943', in D. Bankier and I. Gutman (eds.), *Nazi Europe and the Final Solution* (Jerusalem: Yad Vashem, 2002).
5   Ibid, p. 555.

he helped negotiate the Concordat between the Vatican and the Third Reich. On 2 March 1939 he became Pope Pius XII and evaluations of his behaviour in respect of the Holocaust have varied very widely indeed. In the early 1960s a play by Rolf Hochhuth called 'The Deputy' depicted the Pope as aloof from Jewish suffering. The basic interpretation has been repeated in a number of recent academic studies.[1] By complete contrast, when Pius XII died in 1958 the then Israeli Foreign Minister, Golda Meir, telegraphed the Vatican to pay tribute to his support for Jews during the Holocaust. There have been moves within the Vatican to have Pius XII beatified. Where does the truth lie?

Martin Gilbert and William Rubinstein have both made thoughtful cases supportive of Pius XII.[2] Gilbert points out that the Pope's stance on race was deeply resented by Nazi authorities. After his 1942 Christmas message, in which Pius XII spoke of people being persecuted solely on account of their origins, a report by the Reich Security Head Office said:

> In a manner never known before, the Pope has repudiated the National Socialist New European Order.... Here he is virtually accusing the German people of injustice to the Jews, and makes himself the mouthpiece of the Jewish war criminals.

It is also said that when, after the fall of Mussolini, German-sponsored round ups of Italian Jews began in October 1943, the Pope organised diplomatic protests and instructed that Vatican and Catholic institutions be opened as a safe haven. As a result, of 5,715 Roman Jews named on German deportation lists, 4,715 were hidden around the city. Of these, 477 sheltered in the Vatican itself. Consequently 80% of the city's Jews survived the war. Apparently Jews also hid on the Pope's estate in the north of the country and he sanctioned monasteries to hide them as well. So although 7,000 Italian Jews were deported to death camps, 35,000 were not. A case has also been made that when, in March 1944, steps were taken to round up Jews in Budapest, the Papal Nuncio there, Angelo Rotta, helped organise 40 safe houses in which 25,000

---

[1] These include J. Cornwell, *Hitler's Pope. The Secret History of Pius XII* (London: Viking, 1999) and D. J. Goldhagen, *A Moral Reckoning: The Role of the Catholic Church in the Holocaust and Its Unfulfilled Duty of Repair* (New York: Knopf, 2002).

[2] Accessible essays are available by both authors. See M. Gilbert's review of *The Myth of Hitler's Pope* by D. G. Dalin in *American Spectator*, July–August 2006 (http://www.spectator.org/dsp_article.asp?art_id=10237. Consulted 21 February 2007) and W. D. Rubinstein's review of *Hitler's Pope* by J. Cornwell in *First Things*, January 2000 (http://www.firstthings.com/article.php3?id_article=2496. Consulted 21 February 2007).

people hid. The Vatican protested over the persecutions in Nazi occupied states such as Slovakia too.

Rubinstein fills out the picture. Although he acknowledges that many Catholics thought there were too many Jews in Europe, nonetheless they were against violent persecution. As a result, Catholicism did inhibit Nazi policies. So while 104,000 of 140,000 Jews were deported from the Netherlands which was Protestant, only 28,000 of 90,000 were deported from Catholic Belgium.

Voices such as these, favourable to Pius XI, are however balanced by much more critical ones. It has been said that churchmen should have joined Jews at deportation sites to make clear that they would accompany fellow human beings to death camps. It has also been pointed out that Jozef Tiso, the leader of German-occupied Slovakia, had a background in the Catholic Church but still facilitated the deportation of Jews from his country in 1942. When members of the Jewish underground contacted religious figures around Tiso, such as Archbishop Kametko, they were rebuffed in anti-Semitic terms.[1] In the light of points like these, Pius XII is blamed for failing to motivate adequate numbers of Catholics and churchmen to save Jews. Despite a plethora of reports submitted to the Vatican about the course of the Holocaust, he said too little about what was happening. Even his December 1942 speech only addressed what was being done in a veiled manner. Apart from that, he seems only to have alluded to the Jewish Question on one other occasion during the war, in a speech to the Sacred College of Cardinals given on 2 June 1943.[2]

Susan Zuccotti denies that Pius XII ever issued a directive urging Catholic churchmen to save Jews.[3] When Church diplomats contacted statesmen about the Jewish Question, for example in Slovakia, they did so only tentatively and lacked impact. Likewise the Pope did not denounce the round up of Rome's Jews on 16 October 1943. Zuccotti concludes that the Catholic Church as an institution led by the Pope was far too inactive. When Catholics saved Jews, they acted on their own initiative, not as members of the Church.

Pius XII's extensive silence over the Holocaust is a big part of the problem. How should we interpret it—as a 'cover' to avoid drawing attention to Catholic churchmen trying to save Jews, or as a sign of indifference? In 2000, the Vatican set up a commis-

---

1   J. T. Pawlikowski, 'The Holocaust: Failure in Christian Leadership?', in A. Grobman and D. Landes (eds.), *Critical Issues of the Holocaust* (Dallas, Texas: Rossell Books, 1983), p. 293.
2   S. Zuccotti, 'The Rescue of Jews in Italy and the Existence of a Papal Directive', in Bankier and Gutman (eds.), *Nazi Europe and the Final Solution*, p. 525.
3   Ibid, p. 521. Her book on the topic is S. Zuccotti, *Under his Very Window: the Vatican and the Holocaust in Italy* (Yale, 2002).

sion of six historians to investigate its published documents about the conduct of Pius XII. They produced an interim report and then, apparently, never met again.[1] Their report emphasises the extent of information flowing into the Vatican from locations such as Ukraine, Poland, Vichy France, Hungary, Croatia and even Berlin, but then says that the Vatican's public documentation provides too little information about the responses of the Pope and those around him to it. So on the basis of the available evidence, these scholars could not reach a conclusion about the Pope's behaviour. They could not decide, for instance, how he balanced the persecution of Jews against the reality that very many Catholics were members of the Axis states and, moreover, they were engaged in a battle against the anti-religious Soviet Union. Was the Pope anxious to save lives? Did he want to avoid alienating members of his congregation? Or was he hoping the Axis would defeat Communism? The Vatican has not yet, apparently, made additional documents available. Unfortunately this failure suggests that a fuller picture might not be flattering to either Pius XII or those around him.

4.5 Allied statesmen

Like the Pope, Allied statesmen have been criticised for a lack of response to the Holocaust. Western democracies have been damned for failing to facilitate Jewish emigration. It has been said that, fearing the rise of anti-Semitism, countries such as Britain and the USA limited immigration by the strict application of quotas and refused to launch special projects to save German Jews in particular. It is also pointed out that during the Second World War Shanghai took in more Jewish refugees than Canada, Australia, New Zealand, South Africa and India combined

Once mass killing was underway in Eastern Europe, Allied statesmen probably got the picture of what was happening quite quickly. On 2 June 1942, for instance, the British Minister of Information, Brendan Bracken, and Polish Deputy Prime Minister, Stanislaw Mikolajczyk, talked on BBC about 'the beginning of the wholesale extermination of the Jews.' In fact, Richard Breitman has shown that signals intelligence allowed British government circles to understand that Germany was depopulating the East a good three months before the Wannsee conference. Unfortunately, Breitman also observes that government offices tended to hoard such information rather than

---

1   A copy of their report can be found via the web site 'Jewish–Christian Relations' at http://www.jcrelations.net/en/?id=759. Consulted 21 February 2007.

use it to save lives.¹

D. S. Wyman has offered a fuller critique of how Allied governments reacted to knowledge of persecution. He says that during the Second World War they could 'almost certainly' have saved 'several hundred thousand' lives without compromising the war effort.² Sadly, however, he says that Britain and the USA wanted to avoid a refugee problem and implemented policies to dampen possible public demands for action. Proposals for rescue were brushed aside and authorities set up to deal with the needs of refugees were given too little scope for action. Under the circumstances it was hardly surprising that, later in the war, the US State Department rejected several appeals to bomb Auschwitz. In addition, the USA and Britain failed to exert pressure on Axis satellite countries to release Jews, failed to identify safe havens for them, failed to fund escape attempts and failed to disseminate enough information about what was really going on.

The condemnation sounds as bad as that facing the Pope, but historians have taken issue with it as well—and with more success. Walther Lacqueur is probably right, for instance, that no matter what the Allies had tried to do, they were in no position to save anyone in 1942.³ In fact they could not have saved anyone in 1941 either. Hitler's empire was at its zenith and the USA did not enter the conflict until December of that year. In this situation, Britain was just too hard pressed militarily and, as William Rubinstein has pointed out forcefully, in no position to help people who were actually Hitler's prisoners.⁴

Rubinstein also disagrees that the West made emigration difficult in the 1930s. Even in 1939 the idea of emigration to Palestine was not popular among Jews themselves. Otherwise he says that between 1933 and 1939, 72% of all German Jews (including 83% of German Jewish youth) manage to emigrate. In the 18 months after *Anschluss*, 120,000 of Austria's 185,000 Jews did so too. He says that Anglo–Jewry was active and generous in the support offered to Jewish refugees from Central Europe (a point backed up by Shatzkes) and adds that in the first six months of 1939, 91,780 people entered the UK from Germany and Austria whereas just 191 were refused entry. Between 1 July 1933 and 30 June 1942, 161,051 Jews migrated to the USA, i.e. 35.5% of all the migrants settling there in that period.⁵

---

1   R. Breitman, *Official Secrets. What the Nazis Planned. What the British and Americans Knew* (London: Allen Lane, 1998), pp. 92–7 and 176.
2   D. S. Wyman, 'The Abandonment of the Jews', in Niewyk (ed.), *The Holocaust*, p. 256.
3   W. Laqueur, 'The Failure to Comprehend', in Niewyk (ed), *The Holocaust*, p. 279.
4   W. D. Rubinstein, *The Myth of Rescue* (London: Routledge, 1997), p. 79.
5   Ibid, pp. 77, 29 and 33–35. See also P. Shatzkes, *Holocaust and Rescue. Impotent or Indifferent?*

So should Auschwitz have been bombed? This only became possible after December 1943 when the US army captured Foggia airbase in northern Italy. Although historians have suggested that perhaps low level bombers could have been used to destroy extermination camps, during the war years no one made this proposal at an appropriate point. Even Jewish organisations were unsure whether bombing would help; after all there was a real danger that bombs would kill Jews without stopping the extermination process. When, in October and November 1944, Jewish groups in the USA began calling for Auschwitz to be bombed (and the US Air Force was bombing industrial locations nearby) it was too late in the day since gassing there was halted on 29 November 1944 anyway. It is not even certain that attempts to bomb railway sites would have seriously disrupted the transportation of Jews from Hungary to Auschwitz in 1944 because there were seven possible rail routes. Consequently Rubinstein concludes that there was nothing that the Allies could have done to save Jewish lives.[1]

Nonetheless an impression persists that Allied countries did not quite respond to the Jewish Question properly. Tony Kushner is not alone in maintaining that there were inhibitions on British engagement here.[2] He says the Ministry of Information decided as early as 1941 not to over-emphasise Jewish suffering compared to the universal hardships of the war, hence the British public probably failed to understand fully what was going on. It has also been said that Winston Churchill was very much exercised by the Jewish Question personally, but officials around him lacked the imagination and passion to promote a suitable response to it.[3] Overall, then, there was an official reluctance to risk turning the conflict into a war to save Europe's Jews. As Pamela Shatzkes puts it, in the end the government was 'inevitably indifferent to the fate of a foreign ethnic minority at a time of national emergency.'[4]

The all-consuming mission for London and Washington was to fight the war to a successful conclusion. Given that Allied statesmen were unsure whether they could do this until well into 1943, they refused to be 'diverted' by even the Holocaust. When all is said and done, it is impossible not to have some understanding for their

---

Anglo-Jewry 1938–1945 (Basingstoke: Palgrave, 2002), p. 239.
1   Rubinstein, *Myth of Rescue*, pp. xix, 3, 157–81 and 216.
2   T. Kushner, 'Different Worlds. British Perceptions of the Final Solution during the Second World War', in D. Cesarani (ed.), *The Final Solution. Origins and Implementation* (London: Routledge, 1994), pp. 258–61.
3   B. Wasserstein, *Britain and the Jews of Europe 1939–1945* (Oxford: Clarendon Press, 1979), p. 345.
4   Shatzkes, *Holocaust and Rescue*, p. 239.

position. Indeed, ultimately the fate of Jews in the world also required that Hitler's regime be defeated decisively. But with this said, there is still a residual feeling that perhaps the Allies should have spoken out more clearly, in better time, and more often about what was happening in the East. Indeed, perhaps they should have been more vocal about the persecution of Germany's Jews well before this point.

4.6 Conclusion

Where does all this leave blame and the bystanders? We have seen there were different kinds of collaboration by various populations under Nazi control which facilitated genocide. The behaviour varied (from 'looking the other way' to participation in murder) and the motives did too (from hatred to despair), but fewer 'spanners' than we might have hoped were thrown into the 'works' of the Nazi machine. More forceful statements by international leaders such as the Pope and Allied statesmen should have been made, not least in an attempt to disquiet the populations among whom dreadful events were occurring. They could well have made more people think twice about participating in atrocity or failing to offer help to victims. They would certainly have offered moral support to the brave souls already committed to helping Jews survive.

Chapter 5 The victims' view of the world

5.1 Introduction

Any Jews living on territory controlled by Hitler were in a uniquely hopeless position, but nevertheless some responded in heroic ways that are very well known today. Anne Frank was born in Frankfurt am Main in 1929. Four years later her family left Germany for the Netherlands when her father decided to re-locate his business on account of rising anti-Semitism.[1] Of course the *Wehrmacht* invaded Holland in 1940 and subsequently, on 5 July 1942, the family was served with papers ordering its deportation to the East. At that point the Franks went into hiding, their accommodation being an unused annex in the building that housed the family firm. They stayed there for two years, with young Anne looking out of a sole window at a large chestnut tree. Unfortunately in August 1944 they were betrayed and Anne eventually died of typhus in Bergen-Belsen camp early in 1945. During her long period in hiding, Anne Frank wrote her famous diary.[2]

Rather different was the statement issued by a Jewish underground group in Vilnius ghetto. This was written following the mass execution of the region's Jews in the first few months of the German occupation. Over 30,000 of Vilnius's 60,000 Jews had been killed in the nearby Ponary forests. In January 1942, a Zionist[3] youth group made the following declaration:

> All the roads of the Gestapo lead to Ponary. And Ponary is death! Doubters! Cast off all illusions. Your children, your husbands, and your wives are no longer alive. Ponary is not a camp—all are shot there. Hitler aims to destroy all the Jews of Europe. The Jews of Lithuania are fated to be the first in line. Let us not go as sheep to the slaughter! It is true that we are weak and defenceless, but resistance is the only reply to the enemy! Brothers! It is better to fall

---

1 Interesting web sites about Anne Frank can be found at http://www.annefrank.com and http://www.annefrank.org.
2 Anne Frank, *The Diary of a Young Girl* (London: Penguin, 1997).
3 Zionist – a movement promoting the creation of a Jewish homeland in Palestine.

as free fighters than to live by the grace of the murderers. Resist! To the last breath.'[1]

This was the first time a Jewish source stated unambiguously that the Nazis wanted to annihilate their national group completely. It was also the first Jewish call for armed resistance. From the victims' perspective, first it took courage to accept the extent of Hitler's ambitions and, second, to publicise it. True, the statement must have destroyed the hopes nursed by many people of seeing loved ones again. It must also have left some wondering how to balance responsibilities towards dependent family members with the need to resist occupation authorities. Nonetheless, on this occasion simply facing reality was a brave thing to do.

So what generalisations should we make about more typical responses of Jewish communities to Nazism? Notwithstanding the fact that they have come from Jewish authors, many evaluations actually have been pretty critical. Hannah Arendt judged that Jewish resistance to persecution was 'pitifully small ... incredibly weak and essentially harmless.'[2] No doubt she had in mind that the deaths of six million people could not have happened if Jews had been determined to make their persecutors' job as difficult as possible at every turn. Despite the heroics of a few, too many did too little and so, to put things harshly, helped precipitate their own demise. This line has been argued most famously by Raul Hilberg in *The Destruction of the European Jews*.

Hilberg proposed there were five possible ways Jewish communities could have reacted to the Nazism.[3] They could have resisted the threat, alleviated it, evaded the danger or become paralysed; they could also have complied with Nazism's demands. Hilberg maintained that Europe's Jews displayed minimal efforts at resistance. They had no continent-wide resistance organisation, no general plan for armed action, not even a scheme for a propaganda campaign against Hitler's government. When Jews did try to do something about persecution, Hilberg said it was a matter of 'alleviation.' They tried to make their situation better by writing petitions to Hitler's government in the hope that he could be persuaded to modify its course. But Hilberg judged this strategy a failure, saying 'Everywhere the Jews pitted words against rifles, dialectics against force, and everywhere they lost.'[4] Worse still, Hilberg maintained the most

---

1 Quoted in Y. Gutman, 'The Battles of the Ghettos', in A. Grobman and D. Landes (eds.), *Critical Issues of the Holocaust* (Dallas, Texas: Rossell Books, 1983), pp. 191–2.
2 H. Arendt quoted in Y. Suhl (ed.), *They Fought Back. The Story of the Jewish Resistance in Nazi Europe* (London: MacGibbon and Kee, 1968), p. 16.
3 The relevant discussion can be found in R. Hilberg, *The Destruction of the European Jews* (New York: New Viewpoints, 1973), pp. 662–9.
4 Ibid, p. 664.

common response to Nazism was 'compliance.' Jews organised their own forced labour ahead of Nazi demands and requisitioned valuables from their own communities. They tried to 'tame' the Germans as if dealing with a 'wild beast' in the hope that their hatred would burn itself out.[1] Admittedly the Jewish position reflected 2,000 years of history. They had a long experience of persecution and always had managed to survive. Unfortunately they did not realise they were facing a completely different order of threat and their strategy never stood a chance. They only managed to make the 'ordeal bearable, to make death easy.'[2]

Was Hilberg being fair? An answer requires us to get to grips with the mental world of Central and Eastern European Jews as they experienced the rise of Nazism.

5.2 Germany's Jewish citizens

Germany's Jews were hit hard by the boycotts of 1933. At a stroke they became strangers in their own land.[3] They comprised roughly 500,000 souls or 0.76% of the German population. Although 20% of their number were Orthodox Jews who had arrived in Germany after the First World War, most had roots in the country stretching back much further and were deeply assimilated into national life. It was appropriate that really they thought of themselves as Germans who just happened to be Jewish. As if to prove the point, 30,000 German Jews were awarded Iron Crosses during the First World War for their brave defence of the Fatherland.[4] Moreover, they were largely a respectable, middle class set of individuals who were over-represented in professions such as finance, law, medicine and publishing. They lived mostly in urban centres—70% in towns and cities as a whole and 33% in Berlin alone.[5] How could a group like this have made sense of the rise of Hitler in 'their' Germany?

Some, such as the famous banker Max Warburg, thought Hitler was too vulgar to last. This senior member of the *Reichsbank* ignored warnings from family and friends about Nazism's threat. Perhaps feeling secure because of his considerable social status, he assumed this was a temporary storm that would soon blow over.[6] His atti-

---

1   Ibid, p. 666.
2   Ibid, p. 668.
3   For more information on Germany's Jews, see M. Housden, *Resistance and Conformity in the Third Reich* (London: Routledge, 1997), chapter 6.
4   A. S. Lindemann, *Anti-Semitism before the Holocaust* (London: Longman, 2000), p. 7.
5   M. Kaplan, 'Jewish Women in Nazi Germany', in *Feminist Studies* 16 (1990) pp. 580–1.
6   A. J. Sherman, 'Eine Jüdische Bank in der Ära Schacht', in A. Paucker (ed.), *Die Juden im Nationalsozialistischen Deutschland. 1933–43* (Tübingen: J.C.B. Mohr, 1986).

tude was replicated in many of Germany's Jewish communities. Disbelief at the level of hatred expressed in Nazism coupled with a sense of patriotism motivated self-confident appeals to the government to re-think its Jewish policy. When moves began to exclude Jews from service in the *Wehrmacht*, Jewish veterans protested.[1] Their words fell on deaf ears and on 25 July 1935 Jews were excluded from Germany's armed services completely. More successful, temporarily at least, were the Jews of Upper Silesia. Due to the terms of the peace settlement, the League of Nations had an interest in how national minorities were treated in the area. When anti-Semitic laws were introduced, they complained to the League and the German government suspended the measures. Unfortunately even this victory was short lived because the League's mandate in Upper Silesia expired in 1937 and thereafter the area's Jews suffered the same fate as those in the rest in Germany.[2]

In response to Nazism, German Jewish communities began orgainsing for mutual support in a way they had never done before, not least setting up the nationwide Reich Association of German Jews in September 1933. This functioned until its committee members were deported to Theresienstadt camp in 1943. Very many Jews were also courageous enough, like Anne Frank's family, to leap into the unknown and emigrate. Since Hitler's regime imposed colossal emigration taxes on Jews (they reached 96% in 1939), the massive step meant leaving both friends and economic assets behind. In fact, it meant a complete break with everything people had built up across their lives. Still, between 1933 and 1937, 130,000 German Jews (almost 20% of their number) emigrated. Another 118,000 left after the 'Crystal Night' riots. By October 1941, only 164,000 were left, and half of them were aged over 50.[3]

Naturally a few German Jews took direct action against the Third Reich. Some were active in dissident Socialist and Communist groups, others acted alone—perhaps leaving anti-Nazi leaflets in ideological books found in libraries. Most remarkable of all, however, were the efforts of the Herbert Baum group. These were young committed Communists who worked in the Siemens factory in Berlin during the war. In May 1942 they set fire to the anti-Soviet exhibition 'The Soviet Paradise' which Josef Goebbels had organised in the city's *Lustgarten*.[4] This spectacular act of resistance led to the detection of Baum himself and his execution following a prolonged Gestapo interrogation.

---

[1] See Y. Arad *et al* (eds.), *Documents on the Holocaust* (Oxford: Pergammon, 1981), pp. 71–2.
[2] K. Jonca, 'Jewish Resistance to Nazi Racial Legislation in Silesia, 1933–1937', in F. R. Nicosia and L. D. Stokes (eds.), *Germans against Nazism* (Oxford: Berg, 1990).
[3] Housden, *Resistance and Conformity*, pp. 124–5.
[4] B. Mark, 'The Herbert Baum Group', in Suhl (ed.), *They Fought Back*.

Deportations to the East from Germany started in autumn 1942. Rumours soon got back to Germany of the horrid conditions awaiting people there, and so some decided to go into hiding.[1] Of course this action showed a difficulty facing Jews: they could not hide on their own, they needed the assistance of 'Aryans' with groups of friends who could help in lots of necessary ways (for instance by finding different hiding places and gaining access to food coupons). Hiding was difficult, but some managed it. Mark Roseman relates the tale of Marianne Ellenbogen who survived with a string of opposition-minded German families.[2] For two years she never stayed in the same place longer than three weeks. All in all, about 1,402 Jews managed to survive the war in hiding in Berlin alone.[3] The number was far from negligible.

5.3 Life in the ghettos

The Holocaust, of course, was a continent-wide phenomenon and German Jews were not the only victims. Deportation meant their fate became inter-twined with that of all the other Jews living in ghettos and camps on Polish territory in particular. But Polish Jews had been suffering from almost the minute German troops invaded their country, and Jews in the Soviet Union had similar experiences from the start of Operation Barbarossa.

Ghettoisation began with Reinhard Heydrich's order of 21 September 1939 to concentrate all Jews in occupied Poland near larger railway stations. Ghettos began to be formed in earnest early the next year.[4] Eventually about 200 were created in Central and Eastern Europe, but the Nazis followed no single policy about setting them up and then sealing them. Łódź ghetto was created between February and April 1940. It held about 200,000 people and in due course was sealed off from the outside world completely. Warsaw ghetto was home to over 350,000 Jews and was created more gradually before being sealed in November 1940. Even then, however, it was not closed as securely as Łódź.

Likewise the ghettos were managed by Jewish councils in different ways. These councils, or *Judenräte*, had been established to run the ghettos based on Heydrich's

---

1 For rumours about conditions in the East, see V. Klemperer, *I shall bear Witness: The Diaries of Victor Klemperer 1933–1941* (London: Phoenix, 1999) pp. 537–42.
2 M. Roseman, *The Past in Hiding* (London: Penguin, 2000).
3 K. Kwiet, 'To Leave or not to Leave', in W. H. Pehle (ed.), *November 1938* (Oxford: Berg, 1991), p. 150.
4 S. Beinfeld, 'Life in the Ghettos of Eastern Europe', in Grobman and Landes (eds.), *Critical Issues of the Holocaust*, pp. 173–5.

order of 21 September. In places such as Łódź and Vilnius, a single strong personality tended to dominate proceedings (Chaim Rumkowski in the former, Jacob Gens in the latter), while other ghettos were more 'democratic.' It is worth mentioning, incidentally, that the *Judenräte* sometimes presided over very large administrations indeed. In early 1942 the Łódź *Judenrat* had 12,880 'staff.'[1] These generally included a Jewish police force supposed to enforce the *Judenrat*'s decisions.

Ghettos were little better than prisons for Jews—and very crude prisons at that. They were created in the most run down parts of cities and were under-provisioned in every possible respect. Accommodation was hopelessly overcrowded and, on average, 13 people lived in every room in the Warsaw ghetto. Food was dramatically scarce. People received as little as 184 calories per day (the actual requirement is about 2,500) and so, unsurprisingly, there are recollections of individuals seeing two or three people per day simply drop dead on the street from hunger.[2] In winter, ghettos received virtually no fuel. These were conditions in which typhus thrived. Since ghettos also lacked basic medical facilities, as many as 20% of those who died there did so from natural causes.

In ghettos, Nazis created conditions so severe they were tailored to breaking the human spirit. Under the circumstances, there is an argument for saying that everything done to keep this spirit alive, indeed everything done just to survive, amounted to a kind of resistance. Chaim Kaplan was a Jewish teacher who lived in the Warsaw ghetto. He said this in his diary:

> Lord God! Where do all these people find the money to support themselves? Any form of business or profession is forbidden to them. All businesses have been liquidated; all positions which yielded an income have been abolished; thousands of out-of-work officials roam the streets of Warsaw; there is no [economic sector] apart from grocery stores, which can manage to exist; everything has been shut and closed down, smashed and shattered; all sources of income are blocked; and to top it all a life of shame and humiliation; for there are streets whose right or left sidewalk is forbidden to Jews, and a notice in enormous letters informs one of this. Nevertheless, the multitude lives; the multitude is alert; the multitude declares the conqueror's decrees null and void as the dust of the earth, and does everything in its power to hoodwink

---

1 Ibid, p. 175.
2 Ibid, p. 177. Also L. Steinberg, *Not as a Lamb* (Farnborough: Saxon House, 1970), p. 197. For an interesting memoir of life in a ghetto, see H. Birenbaum, *Hope is the Last to Die. A Coming of Age under Nazi Terror* (New York: M.E. Sharpe, 1996 edition).

him and to deceive him, and to carry out all its activities secretly and indirectly, and God supplies it with sustenance.[1]

Among others, the *Judenräte* of Vilnius, Kaunas and Bialystok all encouraged secret cultural events which were supposed to nurture morale. In Vilnius, the *Judenrat* collected a massive library of books for ghetto residents. Religious services were maintained as much as possible and schools were set up. Ghettos also had thriving underground publishers of every political complexion which generally attempted to politicise the Jewish population.

This is not a trivial point: when conditions are being tailored towards destruction, maintaining the will to survive is not a negligible thing. The trouble was that these efforts to normalise life could only ever go so far. Conditions were so severe that, sooner or later, life had to become a brutal struggle of each against all. People could envy whatever someone else had and, perhaps most depressing of all, when there was a 'lucky break,' generally it was at the expense of someone else.

Life in the ghettos inevitably involved dealing with corruption. Perhaps 80% of the food that entered the Warsaw ghetto did so illegally—by smuggling or bribing guards.[2] Corruption helped people survive, but there had to be a personal cost. Halina Birenbaum's memoir depicts her mother as a strong figure. While her father accepted deportation to Treblinka, her mother bribed her way out of the deportation site. Then she bribed her way into a job at a factory making *Wehrmacht* uniforms. She even bought hiding places in a bunker during the Warsaw ghetto uprising. The woman must have been a force for life—she seems to have been motivated by a desire to survive in order to see her persecutors' defeated—but at what cost in the end? Every time she saved herself and her daughter, someone else filled their places.[3]

These comments, incidentally, are not intended to be criticisms of Birenbaum's mother. They are just supposed to underline how, in the world created by the Nazis, even attempts at survival were hard to untangle from ideas about guilt at behaving in ways that (in a more satisfactory world) were not quite right. This problem was also evident in the work of the *Judenräte*.

1　Entry of 24 April 1940. Quoted in Y. Gutman, 'The Ghettos', in Grobman and Landes (eds.), *Critical Issues of the Holocaust*, p. 169.
2　Ibid, p. 170.
3　Birenbaum, *Hope is the Last to Die*, pp. 29–30, 34, 36 and 58. Birenbaum's mother died at an extermination camp in Lublin, pp. 75–8.

5.4 Leadership and choice

Johnathan Glover is quite right that Nazism assaulted people with moral dilemmas.[1] It gave them terrible problems which they could never solve properly. Even going along with the regime's demands only brought temporary relief—particularly if you were Jewish. Some Jews thought that collaboration might enable them to survive. The group called 'Thirteen' was an extreme case in point. It existed in the Warsaw ghetto and provided information to the Gestapo, for example about the black market, in the wrong-headed hope of being allowed to live.[2]

'Thirteen' practiced a clear kind of collaboration, but what about the *Judenräte*? The people who initially staffed them believed they would be able to represent their communities' interests to the German authorities. It is equally certain that the Nazis only ever saw the committees as tools more effectively to implement their policies. Consequently the committee members found themselves having to do things like register people, tax them and provide lists of names for forced labour or transportation. The very fact that *Jewish* personalities presented these policies to ghetto residents did make refusal that much more difficult in the face of otherwise outrageous demands.[3] Hence Hilberg has interpreted the *Judenräte* as, ultimately, control mechanisms operating in German interests. Worse still, he says they added something to the Nazi system which Germans could not have manufactured alone. They did not have adequate manpower and resources to manage so many people so effectively themselves. Consequently the *Judenräte* ended up being valuable collaborators in Hitler's system.

It is easy to see that the *Judenräte* contained many well-meaning men. Leo Baeck had long been a respected member of the leadership of the Reich Association of German Jews and he joined the *Judenrat* at Theresienstadt. But time and again people like him were put in impossible positions. Once, Baeck was told by an escapee from Auschwitz that people were being gassed there. What was Baeck supposed to do with this information? Many of the members of his ghetto were old or infirm. They could not escape or live as partisans in the forests. So Baeck kept quiet in order not to worry helpless people over information that had come to him as a rumour.[4]

A comparable dilemma faced Rudolf Kastner in Hungary. He was not a member

---

1. J. Glover, *Humanity. A Moral History of the Twentieth Century* (London: Jonathan Cape, 1999), pp. 381–2.
2. Y. Bauer, *Rethinking the Holocaust* (Yale, 2001), p. 145.
3. Hilberg, *Destruction*, p. 114.
4. L. Baker, *Days of Sorrow* (New York: Macmillan, 1978), p. 137.

of a *Judenrat* but was a Hungarian Jew who negotiated with Nazi authorities in Budapest in 1944.[1] He managed to have 21,000 Hungarian Jews sent to a camp near Vienna where they survived the war. He also had another 1,684 Jews put on a train out of Hungary. These eventually were transported to Switzerland. Nonetheless, after the war Kastner was criticised heavily by some people in Israel, particularly by relatives of those he did not save. He was said to have 'played God' with people's lives and was assassinated on 3 March 1957.

Returning to a discussion of the *Judenräte*, some may have restrained the growth of serious Jewish resistance. In general terms, influential members of the *Judenräte* provided rationalisations in favour of accepting Nazi policies. Hence Rumkowski in Łódź said survival required the ghetto to work hard in German interests.[2] You can also find evidence of members of various *Judenräte* complaining that ghetto inhabitants were not respecting curfews, not keeping their ghetto clean, not wearing their Yellow Star properly, not turning up for work duties—so on and so forth.[3] More specifically, the Jewish committees lived under the threat of German authorities exerting collective reprisals against innocent members of the whole community if underground groups were found to be active in their communities. As a result, often they were anxious not to encourage, for instance, underground presses or the stockpiling of weapons.[4] In other words, Jews ended up controlling Jews.

In a sense, Jewish attempts to manage their communities in a way acceptable to Nazi authority also deflected resistance groups from where their real targets lay. Taking occupied Belgium as an example, the Jewish leadership in this country tried to mediate between its community and the Nazis. Consequently it organised forced labour and deportations itself. As a result, however, Jewish resistance figures decided that they had to deal with Jewish managers before they could take direct action against Nazi authorities. Hence Jewish resisters targeted Jews working on behalf of German interests, not Nazi administrators. In fact they shot the Jew organising forced labour in August 1942.[5] Comparably, in Warsaw ghetto the resistance first had to subvert the

---

[1] Details of his actions can be found in Bauer, *Rethinking the Holocaust*. pp. 227–9 and S.S. Friedman, *A History of the Holocaust* (London: Vallentine Mitchell, 2004), pp. 363–4. Also http://www.kasztnermemorial.com.

[2] I. Trunk, 'Why the Jewish Councils Cooperated', in D. L. Niewyk (ed.), *The Holocaust: Problems and Perspectives of Interpretation* (Boston: Houghton Mifflin, 1997), p. 133.

[3] Y. Arad, I. Gutman and A. Margaliot (eds.), *Documents on the Holocaust* (Jerusalem: Yad Vashem, 1996), pp. 263–3.

[4] G. D. Draenger, *Justyna's Narrative* (Amherst: Uni. of Massachusetts Press, 1996), p. 24.

[5] M. Steinberg, 'The Jews in the Years 1940–1944: Three Strategies for Coping with a Tragedy', in D. Michman (ed.), *Belgium and the Holocaust: Jews, Belgians, Germans* (Jerusalem: Yad

authority of the *Judenrat* before it could properly become active. Only then could resisters move around freely.[1]

It can be argued that Jews were dealt with more brutally when no Jewish committee existed, also that the members of the *Judenräte* acted to mitigate suffering and in the hope that they would help some of their people survive. Without doubt they also faced extremely difficult choices. In the end, however, attempts to compromise with Nazism were doomed. They were a distraction from the ground where resistance ultimately had to lie.

5.5 Making opportunities to escape and resist

Against all the odds, some people did escape life in the ghetto. A recent study of Jews in Warsaw proposes that between 2 and 5% of the city's Jews went into hiding. Paulsson suggests that about 28,000 Jews were living clandestine lives somewhere in the city at any given time. This meant that Warsaw had the largest hidden Jewish population in Europe. Apparently escapees had about a 40% chance of survival, a figure that was about the same for Jews who went into hiding in Western Europe. Interestingly the author also surmises that so many people must have required the assistance of between 70,000 and 90,000 Poles.[2]

Eventually underground organisations grew up in most ghettos. They forged papers, established their own presses and used female couriers to maintain contact with each other.[3] They also initiated armed action, a feat which was far from easy. On the one hand, relatively few ghetto residents had experience of handling arms, never mind staging an insurrection. Often, when they got hold of a gun, younger Jews were more likely to shoot themselves than a Nazi soldier or policeman.[4] On the other hand, it was hard to find weapons. Underground ghetto groups had to contact Polish partisans and persuade them to hand over weapons. Given that many Polish partisans hated Jews almost as much as Germans, there was a problem here.[5] Despite all these

---

    Vashem, 1998), p. 364.
1   Y. Bauer, 'The Judenräte—Some Conclusions', in *Patterns of Jewish Leadership in Nazi Europe 1933–1945. Proceedings of the Third Yad Vashem International Historical Conference 4–7 April 1977* (Jerusalem: Yad Vashem, 1979), p. 395.
2   G. S. Paulsson, *Secret City: the Hidden Jews of Warsaw, 1940–1945* (Yale, 2002), pp. 2, 5, 56 and 231.
3   For stories about couriers, see B. Gurewitsch, *Mothers, Sister, Resisters: Oral Histories of Women who survived the Holocaust* (Suscaloosa: Uni of Alabama Press, 1998), pp. 222–8.
4   Draenger, *Justyna's Narrative*, p. 25.
5   S. Krakowski, 'The Polish Underground and the Jews in the Years of the Second World War', in D.

difficulties, uprisings did occur in at least 20 ghettos in Eastern Europe.¹ The first was in Vilnius in early 1942. Most famous of all, however, was the Warsaw ghetto uprising. When the last residents realised their home was being liquidated, they began an armed action which lasted from 19 April to 16 May 1943. About 750 Jewish fighters had to be pacified by between 2,000 and 3,000 German troops—men the Nazis could ill—afford so soon after the battle of Stalingrad.

5.6 Death camps and attempts to survive them

Armed resistance also occurred in at least 5 extermination camps.² To understand how remarkable this was, first we have to say a word about the conditions found there. Jews were transported to the camps in inhuman conditions and often experienced a traumatic arrival. Many, most notably those who arrived at Bełżec, Chełmno, Sobibór and Treblinka, were killed quickly—tricked into gas chambers where they expected to have a shower.³ Otherwise they faced a massive physical and psychological assault. They could be beaten by camp functionaries, terrorised by dogs, divided from their families, forced out of their own clothes into camp outfits and have their heads shaved so they could not even recognise people they knew well. If anyone tried to resist, camp authorities imposed dreadful collective punishments. If, say, a Jew assaulted the guards then he, his family and an arbitrary additional number of Jews would be killed.⁴

Once in a camp, inmates had to fight to survive. They would steal each other's food and blankets. Massive numbers contracted disease. Survival could depend on cunning. For example when one woman hurt her foot, rather than be spotted limping on account of injury and risk selection for death, she broke the heel off one of her shoes.⁵ In the chaos, people did sometimes make a close friend and, just occasionally, individuals would cover for each other if someone became sick— sometimes they even took punishment on behalf of a friend. Equally some camp inmates were buoyed up by religious belief or a burning desire to survive to bear testimony to the world.

    Bankier and I. Gutman (ed.), *Nazi Europe and the Final Solution* (Jerusalem: Yad Vashem, 2003), p. 227.
1   Grobman and Landes (eds.), *Critical Issues of the Holocaust*, p. 191.
2   Ibid.
3   H. Friedlander and S. Milton, 'Surviving', in Grobman and Landes (eds.), *Critical Issues of the Holocaust*, p. 233.
4   A. Grobman, 'Attempts at Resistance in the Camps', in Grobman and Landes (eds.), *Critical Issues of the Holocaust*, p. 250.
5   Birenbaum, *Hope is the Last to Die*, pp. 84–5.

A handful even managed to smuggle themselves out of camps, for instance hidden in piles of clothes loaded onto freight trains.[1] More typically, however, survival in this environment amounted to a lethal game of chance.

Yet even in the midst of all this turmoil, inmates staged uprisings. Some transportations of Jews rioted immediately upon arrival at a camp. This happened at Treblinka on one occasion when a consignment of Jews arrived from Bialystok. It also happened at Sobibór in October 1943 when Jews arrived from Minsk. At Bełżec, the *Sonderkommando* (i.e. Jews used to clear out the gas chambers after everyone was dead) rioted when ordered to deal with a chamber full of women and children.[2] But these were relatively small-scale events.

Larger armed uprisings also occurred, notably toward the end of the Holocaust when the last few remaining captive Jews knew what their fate would be. At Treblinka, inmates got hold of weapons via female couriers and by corrupting their often Ukrainian guards. The latter, incidentally, became increasingly nervous as the Red Army approached the camps. Consequently on 2 August 1943, with the 850 surviving camp inmates fearing they would soon be killed, an uprising broke out. It resulted in about 660 people getting out of the camp and roughly 100 got clean away. On 14 October 1943, a similar event happened at Sobibór. A key participant was a Jew from the Soviet Union who was a prisoner of war, Sash Pechersky. At half past three the inmates began killing German camp staff as they came to a tailor's hut to be fitted for new uniforms. Thereafter they rioted with a few hand guns and axes supplemented by occasional machine guns grabbed from fleeing guards. About 600 people got out of the camp and a third could not be recaptured.[3] On 7 October 1943 there was also a riot among the *Sonderkommando* at Auschwitz and a crematorium was burned down. Although they escaped from the camp, on this occasion no-one survived.

5.7 Jews as partisans

To complete the picture we should recognise that some Jews became partisans. Jewish partisan groups were active in 38 towns and villages in Eastern Europe.[4]

---

1 Y. Arad, *Belzec, Sobibor, Treblinka: The Operation Reinhard Death Camps* (Bloomington: Indiana University Press, 1987), chapter 32.
2 Ibid, pp. 256–7.
3 Arad, *Belzec, Sobibor, Treblinka*, chapters 36 and 37.
4 D. Levin, 'Eastern European Jews in the Partisan Ranks during World War II', in Grobman and Landes (eds.), *Critical Issues of the Holocaust*, p. 212.

Another 30,000 Jews were active among specifically Soviet-backed partisan groups.[1] Relatedly, there were also two large family camps in the forests of Belorussia. One was led by Tuvia Bielski and contained 1,200 people; the other was commanded by Shimon Zorin and held 800.[2] These family camps were a terrific response to persecution and an ambitious project for survival.

5.8 Conclusion

Hilberg was too harsh on Europe's Jews. No doubt they did underestimate Nazism's threat, but they were hardly alone in doing this. If very many indeed did not rebel even at the entrance to the gas chamber, neither did Soviet prisoners of war (trained soldiers) when some of their number were in a similar position.[3] Europe's Jews were far from being a united warrior nation capable of hurling themselves against a massive modern state which found no small amount of support for and collaboration with its racism among the peoples of Nazi occupied Europe. Likewise it might have been possible to set up a family camp for a thousand armed Jews in the forests of Belorussia, but such an option hardly existed in, say, Bavaria or on the outskirts of Paris.

So what was possible under circumstances that were all but impossible? Despite the short comings of the *Judenräte*, perhaps even these were a necessary 'evil.' No doubt the Nazis would have made life that much more painful had the Jews not co-operated. Otherwise, Jews did everything they could: they emigrated, hid, escaped and attempted rebellion. For those who were trapped and had no options left, we should not be surprise that they went to their deaths with as little hardship as possible. They are not the ones who deserve to be criticised.

---

1   This fact underlines how strange it was that Soviet partisans did not do more to disrupt the death camp system.
2   N. Tec, *Defiance: the Bielski Partisans* (OUP, 1993).
3   Grobman, 'Attempts at Resistance in the Camps', pp. 252–3.

Conclusion: the legacy of the Holocaust

6.1 The Holocaust as 'moral resource'

Europe was just not the same after the Holocaust. Before 1939, the central and eastern regions of the continent especially had been home to millions-strong Jewish communities with distinctive cultural characteristics. By 1945 these had gone. In fact, the Holocaust sent out shock waves lasting until the start of the twenty first century. Maurice Papon, a Vichy France administrator responsible for organising the deportation of 1,600 Jews from around Bordeaux, was put on trial only in October 1997. The next year he was sentenced to 10 years' imprisonment and was actually jailed between October 1999 and September 2002, at which point he was freed on account of ill health. He died on 17 February 2007 aged 96. Only in the 1990s were the business dealings of Swiss banks scrutinised sufficiently closely to lead to the publication of lists of assets and accounts which could have belonged to Holocaust victims, and which could be claimed by relatives. The list is still available today.[1] In early 2007 reports were being compiled saying that hundreds of billions of dollars' worth of compensation promised by European states was still outstanding to Holocaust victims and their families.[2]

Some might argue that the Holocaust has actually been gaining in importance with the passage of time. Tony Kushner says that, today, awareness of the Holocaust is more firmly rooted in the liberal democratic cultures of, say, the United Kingdom and the USA than ever before.[3] This is true not only in respect of educational syllabuses, but also of popular literature, film and television. Of course memorials to the Holocaust can be found at very many of the sites you would expect, likewise among many of the populations who had a clear stake in what happened. Naturally in Berlin you can visit the house which held the Wannsee conference and there is an impressive Holocaust museum in the city centre. Likewise in Amsterdam you can see where Anne Frank hid. There are important memorials at Yad Vashem in Jerusalem and at

---

1 In March 2007 the web address was http://www.dormantaccounts.ch/.
2 See the stories carried by *Der Spiegel*. www.spiegel.de/international/0,1518,460901,00.html.
3 T. Kushner, *The Holocaust and the Liberal Imagination* (Oxford: Blackwell, 1994), p. 207.

Auschwitz itself. Riga's Museum of the Occupation of Latvia deals with events in a most memorable fashion. In addition, however, you can find a Holocaust exhibition at the Imperial War Museum, London and there is an impressive United States Holocaust Memorial Museum in Washington, USA. In other words, paying tribute to the Holocaust has become a general obligation. This development has been underlined by the United Nations' decision of November 2005 to establish 27 January as an annual Holocaust remembrance day. This was the date in 1945 when the Red Army arrived at Auschwitz–Birkenau. According to the UN, the purpose of the remembrance day is to help ward off genocide in the future.[1]

To use Jonathan Glover's phrase, the Holocaust has become an important 'moral resource' of the modern world.[2] It is hard to quibble with the sentiment. Such a terrible event provides us with many morality tales supportive of tolerant and compassionate behaviour. But the wide currency of the Holocaust has not always been unproblematic. Just sometimes the search for contemporary relevance or an uplifting message has been pursued to the detriment of understanding the event's historical realities.

When Anne Frank's story began to be marketed widely, some of the more harrowing things she wrote were missed out. For instance, it was turned into a stage play which omitted both her characterisation of Nazis hunting Jews as medieval slavers and her suspicion (based on a BBC broadcast) that Jews were being gassed. Likewise early German versions of the diary played down sections which identified Anne as a German citizen herself. Consequently the text diverted attention from the way Germans had persecuted other Germans.[3] Audiences were given only part of the picture in order to avoid alienating some people and to turn the story into something more uplifting than it already was. Equally, concerns have been expressed over the way some powerful lobby groups (such as Jewish communities in the USA) have started appropriating the Holocaust. Their interest has led to practical pressures to portray the event in some ways rather than others, particularly to establish the genocide of the Jews as without historical parallel.[4]

It is relatively easy to find aphorisms encouraging us always to keep the past in

---

1 http://www.un.org/holocaustremembrance/emainpage.shtml
2 J. Glover, *Humanity. A Moral History of the Twentieth Century* (London: Jonathan Cape, 1999), p. 406.
3 A. H. Rosenfeld, 'Popularization and Memory: the Case of Anne Frank', in P. Hayes (ed.), *Lessons and Legacies. The Meaning of the Holocaust in a Changing World* (Evanston, Illinois: Northwestern University Press, 1991), pp. 254–65.
4 M. R. Marrus, 'The Use and Misuse of the Holocaust', in Hayes (ed.), *Lessons and Legacies.* p. 111.

mind. According to Cicero, anyone who remains ignorant of what happened before they were born will always remain a child; or as Nietzsche put it, 'One must have a good memory to be able to keep the promises one has given.'[1] It falls to students of history to make sure that the stories of the past are told as truthfully as possible. If these are distorted, then the lessons we draw from them are liable to be distorted too.

6.2 Legal legacy. Nuremberg, crimes against humanity and international justice

Not only has the Holocaust left a moral-cultural legacy, it has left a legal heritage too. In 1946 Nuremberg was home to the first ever multinational criminal tribunal. Judges from France, Russia, the USA and the United Kingdom judged crimes committed by 22 senior Nazis. Admittedly key figures were already dead, not least Reinhard Heydrich, Heinrich Himmler, Odilo Globocnik and Adolf Hitler himself. All the same, the likes of Hans Frank (the Governor General), Alfred Rosenberg (racial ideologist) and Julius Streicher (anti-Semitic propagandist) could still be charged for their conduct.

This was a new kind of law court and it dealt with new crimes—most notably 'crimes against humanity.' The creation of such a category of wrong-doing had been discussed in the League of Nations after the First World War. Greek Foreign Minister Nicolas Politis made such a proposal in the light of massacres of Armenians carried out inside the Ottoman Empire in 1917. The initiative proved premature, however. Still, comparable concerns re-emerged during the Second World War when, in 1944, Ralph Lemkin produced a detailed study of Nazi occupation policies and created the word 'genocide' (from the Greek word 'genos'—tribe or people—and the Latin word 'cide'—killing).[2] The Allies already had plans to establish an international tribunal to deal with senior Nazis whose crimes spread across large territories and the idea of 'genocide' fed into their thinking. So when the London Four Powers Agreement was issued on 8 August 1945, it included a charter founding an international military tribunal and a path-breaking set of charges. Senior Nazis would stand trials for conspiracy to wage war, crimes against peace, war crimes and, indeed, crimes against

---

1   Cicero quoted in A. C. Grayling, 'The last word on History', in *The Guardian* 15 January 2000; and Nietzsche quoted in A.R. Eckardt, 'The Christian World goes to Bitburg', in G. H. Hartman (ed.), *Bitburg in Moral and Political Perspective* (Bloomington: Indiana University Press, 1986), p. 82.
2   L. Kuper, *Genocide: Its Political Use in the Twentieth Century* (New Haven: Yale, 1981), p. 22.

humanity. The final charge was defined as follows:

> murder, extermination, enslavement, deportation, and other inhumane acts committed against any civilian population, before or during the war; or persecution on political, racial or religious grounds in execution of or in connection with any crime within the jurisdiction of the Tribunal, whether or not in violation of domestic law of the country where perpetrated.[1]

Many criticisms have been levelled at the Nuremberg tribunal. Some say it was more a matter of the victors exacting vengeance than proper justice. Others say it was a stage set for a morality play in which everything was simplified into a battle of 'Good' against 'Evil.' Others again have pointed out that the defendants were charged with crimes against humanity even though no such 'offence' was defined in law until after the war had ended. If there was no law defining crimes against humanity between 1939 and 1945, how could anyone have broken it?[2] But what was the alternative to the Nuremberg tribunal? Before the decision was taken to establish the court, Churchill estimated that the top 50 or 100 Nazis should be declared outlaws and shot in summary fashion; American sources were talking about 2,500 spontaneous executions; Stalin, however, intended to liquidate between 50,000 and 100,000 Nazi supporters. The tribunal was certainly better than these alternatives and the charges it dealt in surely had to be recognised sooner or later. This was as good a moment as any.

The Nuremberg tribunal at least left the legacy (as an ideal anyway) that conflict should be resolved with a show of justice rather than brute force. It also pointed the way the United Nations would follow. In 1948 that organisation agreed the Convention on the Prevention and Punishment of Genocide which owed a great deal to the work done by the international military tribunal.[3] When the UN later indicted people for atrocities perpetrated in the Yugoslav civil war of the early 1990s, genocide and crimes against humanity featured among the most important charges cited. The UN tribunal dealing with the killing of 100,000s of Tutsis and moderate Hutus in Rwanda-Burundi in 1994 repeated the message that powerful people committing genocide and other outrageous acts would not be allowed to escape justice by the international community. The message has been emphasised by the creation in 2002, under the auspices of the UN, of the permanent International Criminal Court at The

---

1   The London Agreement is reproduced at www.ess.uwe.ac.uk/documents/chtrimt.htm and via www.icrc.org/ihl.nsf/INTRO/350?OpenDocument. See Article 6 for the charges.
2   For a discussion of related themes, see M. Housden, *Hans Frank. Lebensraum and the Holocaust* (Basingstoke: Palgrave, 2003), chapter 11.
3   The text of the convention is available at www.hrweb.org/legal/genocide.html.

Hague. In the post-Holocaust world, even heads of state have become answerable for their conduct. On paper at least, atrocity is intolerable wherever it happens and for whatever supposed reason.[1]

6.3 Legal legacy. National responses

The Holocaust gave impetus to national as well as international legal developments. Admittedly national responses have faced more than a few problems. We already know it took France 52 years before Maurice Papon was held accountable. Before this, he had held a senior position in the French aerospace industry and had begun to develop a high level political career. If Papon re-invented himself in his home country after 1945, others did something similar by fleeing to new parts of the world. In 1961 Adolf Eichmann was put on trial in Jerusalem for his part in the Holocaust, but only after Israeli security personnel kidnapped him from Argentina. Other Nazis found refuge in, for instance, Syria and Egypt.[2]

Problematic responses to former Nazis also occurred closer to home. Trials were instituted against 185 members of, among others, the *Einsatzgruppen* and the Reich Security Head Office. Of these, 25 were executed, 20 sentenced to life and 97 given prison sentences of over 25 years. It is questionable, however, whether the wider process of freeing West Germany from the heritage of Nazism was pressed forward with real determination. De-nazification resulted in only a few being jailed for long periods while a third of suspects were simply acquitted. It proved depressingly easy for German participants in the Holocaust to find good jobs after the war. Franz Six (a liquidation officer active around Smolensk) attained a senior position in Porsche–Diesel, Werner Best (seniors SS officer in Denmark) worked for the Stinnes Foundation, Rudolf Bolgner (an assistant to Adolf Eichmann) got a job with a court in Mannheim, Wilhelm Koppe (a senior SS man from Chełmno and the Government General) worked as a manager in a chocolate factory—the list goes on an on.[3]

More surprising still was the ease with which former perpetrators built homes in the very countries which had opposed Hitler most vigorously. After the Second World War, the British government did not pursue Nazi crimes as firmly as it might have done. By 1948 memoranda written in the Foreign Office were recommending that

---

[1] For further discussion of the development of international justice systems, see G. Robertson, *Crimes against Humanity. The Struggle for Global Justice* (London: Penguin, 2002).
[2] S. S. Friedman, *A History of the Holocaust* (London: Vallentine Mitchell, 2004), p. 387.
[3] Ibid, pp. 385–401.

the past be put behind everyone as quickly as possible.[1] The UK did not introduce domestic legislation dealing with people suspected of committing Nazism's crimes until 1991 when the War Crimes Act came on the statute books. The first prosecution in the UK began only in 1999, against Anthony Sawoniuk. Eventually the 78 year old was sentenced to life imprisonment for killing Jews in the occupied East and died in jail in 2005.[2] Nor was Britain alone in failing to pursue legal action with due diligence. After 1945 the USA opened its doors to refugees from Central and Eastern Europe and at least some people who had done unpleasant things took advantage. They included a number of Ukrainians who had been involved in killing Jews in the Baltic States and beyond.[3]

Despite the fact that individual perpetrators of the Holocaust too often were not pursued with due rigor, the event still has left a mark on liberal democracies in a more general way. As a rule, legislation now exists banning the public dissemination of anything approaching racism. Today most European countries have strict laws designed to constrain any such possibility. In fact no small number of countries, including Germany and Austria, regard attitudes to the Holocaust as a litmus test of racism and have passed laws banning specifically the trivialisation of that event. Germany first passed such legislation in 1985 and tightened it in 1994. Austria has the Prohibition Law. This was the legislation which David Irving broke in 1989 when he delivered a number of speeches in Austria which said, amongst other things, that the gas chambers of Auschwitz were 'a fairytale.' When he returned to Austria in 2005 he was arrested, tried and imprisoned.[4]

6.4 Political legacy. Uses and abuses of history

As the last paragraph makes plain, the Holocaust has left a clear legacy: racist politics has been put beyond the pale. But the political heritage stretches further and can be more controversial.

The state of Israel was established in 1948 after a protracted armed struggle by Jews against the British administration of Palestine. The next year, the Federal Republic

---

[1] I. Cotler (ed), *Nuremberg Forty Years Later. The Struggle against Injustice in our Time* (Montreal and Kingston: McGill–Queen's UP, 1995), p. 46.
[2] For a fuller story of former Nazi functionaries coming to the UK, see D. Cesarani, *Justice Delayed* (London: Orion, 2001).
[3] Friedman, *History of the Holocaust*, pp. 385–401. For the case of John Demjanjuk, see G. Sereny, *The German Trauma. Experiences and Reflections* (London: Allen Lane, 2000), pp. 309–58.
[4] See, for instance, 'Irving jailed for denying Holocaust', in *The Guardian* 21 February 2006.

of Germany (West Germany) was created. There followed a major effort by post-war West German governments to come to terms with this new representative of Jewish interests. In the early 1950s, Konrad Adenaur (Chancellor of West Germany) and Ben Gurion (Prime Minister of Israel) began the process of establishing a system to compensate victims of the Holocaust. Over $100 billion has been paid out by Germany so far by way of compensation and (at the start of the twenty first century) roughly $624 million is paid out annually to survivors in the form of pensions. In addition, no small number of initiatives has been launched to bring Germany and Israel closer together. Since 1965, more than 2 million young Germans and Israelis have participated in educational exchanges. Towns have been twinned between the two countries and the organisation 'Action Reconciliation' has sent volunteers from Germany to Israel to work in, for example, hospitals.[1]

None of this, however, has prevented accusations that the Holocaust sometimes has been abused by even mainstream politicians. M.R.Marrus has noted an increasing inclination on the part of Israeli politicians to invoke Jewish suffering as a means to justifying government policies which otherwise might be subject to extensive criticism.[2] Norman Finkelstein has levelled comparable charges more energetically. He has complained about how the Holocaust has been deployed to 'immunize' Israel from 'legitimate censure.' The Holocaust has been used as a 'ploy to delegitimate all criticism of Jews.' To his mind, arguments that the Holocaust was unique are particularly dangerous because they can be used to imply that a past involving singular persecution provides a basis for a unique kind of entitlement in the present day.[3]

Of course, reactions of mainstream German politicians to the Holocaust have tended to be so careful that it is hard to criticize them in such strident terms. Some German politicians have gone out of their way to make plain the depth of national shame at what happened in Germany's name. Most famously, in December 1970 during a visit to Poland, Federal Chancellor Willy Brandt knelt, head bowed, in front of the memorial to the Warsaw ghetto uprising. His message was unequivocal and in 1971 he received the Nobel Peace Prize.

---

[1] Official information from the German side about efforts to promote reconciliation can be found at www.germany.info/relaunch/info/archives/backgroundpapers2.html and www.germany.info/relaunch/info/archives/background/israel.html. For a suggestion that compensation payments are very much incomplete, see www.spiegel.de/international/0,1518,460901,00.html.

[2] M. R. Marrus, 'The Use and Misuse of the Holocaust', in Hayes (ed.), *The Meaning of the Holocaust*, p. 113.

[3] N. G. Finkelstein, *The Holocaust Industry. Reflections on the Exploitation of Jewish Suffering* (London: Verso, 2000), p. 37, 47 and 95.

Controversy over the place of the Holocaust in German political culture really only became a 'hot potato' in the 1980s. It was a period in which US President Ronald Reagan was pursuing the Cold War enthusiastically. Part of his agenda involved exploring ways in which contemporary Allies against Soviet Communism might be able to develop shared ideas of the past. At the time, Helmut Kohl was Chancellor of West Germany. He represented the conservative Christian Democratic Party and as a young man had written his doctorate about German history. He was very much attuned to promoting an understanding of his nation's past which would enable Germans to feel pride and continuity with former generations.[1] Obviously the Holocaust was a massive stumbling block both to Reagan's aim (since it marked out part of Germany's heritage as criminal) and that of Kohl (how could you feel good about having *that* centre-stage of your history?).

Reagan's visit to West Germany in 1985 was always likely to be an interesting event. He gave a speech at Bitburg military cemetery in which he talked about '... those young men ... fighting in the German uniform, drafted into service to carry out the hateful wishes of the Nazis.' He said they '... were victims just as surely as the victims of the concentration camps.'[2] The provocative nature of the statement was intensified by the fact that not only 2,000 *Wehrmacht* soldiers were buried at Bitburg, but also 47 members of the *Waffen-SS*. Reagan's speech led to a great deal of criticism. Even though the *Waffen-SS* men had not participated in the Holocaust, they were too close to it for comfort. Reagan and Kohl (by virtue of supporting Reagan's sentiments) were accused of wanting to take the Holocaust out of history, attempting to wipe out whole chunks of memory, ignoring the stories of victims and conflating very different kinds of suffering.[3]

On the other hand, there was no question that Reagan publicised issues with which more conservative minds in Germany had sympathy. A feeling was soon being expressed openly that German identity had for too long existed under the shadow of the Nazi period, and especially the Holocaust. This was why young Germans had tended to identify themselves with Europe rather than their home country. But now a historical debate blew up in Germany called the *Historikerstreit* (roughly 'the punch up between historians') about how the Holocaust should be dealt with in the frame-

---

1 J. Habermas, 'Defusing the Past: a Politico-Cultural Tract', in G. H. Hartmann (ed.), *Bitburg in Moral and Political Perspective* (Bloomington: Indiana University Press, 1986), pp. 44–5.
2 A. H. Rosenfeld, 'Another Revision: Popular Culture and the Changing Image of the Holocaust', in Hartman (ed.), *Bitburg*, p. 94.
3 G. H. Hartman, 'Introduction'; M. Merhav, 'Honouring Evil'; and T. W. Adorno, 'What does "coming to terms with the past" mean?' —all in Hartman (ed.), *Bitburg*.

work of the nation's history. Again some conservative voices proved particularly notable. Ernst Nolte argued that Nazism might have involved a defensive reaction against 'Asiatic deeds' perpetrated by Stalin in the Soviet Union and that (apart from the application of gassing technology and its racial character) the Holocaust was in many ways a copy of the class war perpetrated by Bolshevism. Andreas Hillgruber went on to publish a short book one half of which depicted the Holocaust, while the other half described the destruction of Germany at the end of the Second World War. He called the study *Zweierlei Untergang*—'two kinds of downfall.' No small number of historians, as well as other academics, objected strongly to the arguments mounted by Nolte and Hillgruber, but if nothing else the *Historikerstreit* highlighted how very hard it was proving both to locate an event as momentous as the Holocaust in a nation's history and, at the same time, to provide an adequate source of identity for post-war Germans.[1]

But dealing with the Holocaust is not just a particularly difficult issue for Germany; it is still proving hard for other nations involved in its perpetration. After gaining independence from the Soviet Union, Estonia, Latvia and Lithuania all set up historical commissions to investigate the conduct of the Holocaust on their territories.[2] In Lithuania's case, research has led to the discovery of considerable popular participation.[3] It is interesting to notice, however, that the three historical commissions (in admittedly sometimes different ways) all couple the investigation of crimes committed under Nazi occupation (i.e. by Estonians, Latvians and Lithuanians) with those committed under Soviet occupation (i.e. by Soviet authorities against Estonians, Latvians and Lithuanians). Hence the Lithuanian investigative body is called 'The International Commission for the Evaluation of the Crimes of the Nazi and Soviet Occupation Regimes in Lithuania.'[4]

It is also interesting to notice that the desire to equate Stalinist and Nazi crimes has started to filter through to the European Union. Legislative initiatives underway in early 2007 aiming to introduce anti-hate laws across the Union began to spark discussions about whether issues relating to the Communist and Nazi pasts should

---

1 Perhaps the best discussion of the issues raised here is R. J. Evans, *In Hitler's Shadow: West German Historians and the Attempt to Escape from the Nazi Past* (London: I.B.Tauris, 1989).
2 See E-C. Onken, 'The Politics of Finding Historical Truth: Reviewing Baltic History Commissions and their Work', in *Journal of Baltic Studies* 38 (2007) pp. 109–16.
3 See J. Tauber, '"Jews. Your History on Lithuanian Soil is over!" Lithuania and the Holocaust in 1941', in *Central and Eastern European Review* 1 (2007) www.ceer.org.uk.
4 The web site for the organisation is www.komisija.lt/en/. For an idea of how the Holocaust and Soviet crimes are being groups together, see the web site www.am.gov.lv/en/latvia/history/. (Consulted 25 February 2007.) See also Onken, 'The Politics of Finding Historical Truth'.

be dealt with by one unifying law. Estonia, Slovenia and Poland apparently have favoured such equality, while Slovakia has thought it inappropriate.[1] In other words, the political and legal issues attached to the Holocaust are far from finished yet.

6.5 Conclusion. The root of it all—personal legacies

None of this should make us overlook the fact that the Holocaust has left very personal legacies. In no small measure, the political difficulties thrown up by the event are rooted in the extensive personal hurts associated with it. Aaron Hass has studied Holocaust survivors and their children.[2] Taking survivors first, he found a group of people broadly moving forward in their lives, but very much in the shadow of an array of background worries. If anything, increasing age only made their burdens worse, since they had more time to think about the past. This was not a happy prospect for mothers who could remember deciding not to be gassed alongside their daughters, or children who had been unable to say goodbye to their parents. But Hass made it plain that some of this unhappiness was, sadly, passed on to the children of survivors. Parents could easily submit their offspring to moral black mail with phrases such as, 'How could you do this to me, after all I have suffered?'

And if too many perpetrators of the Holocaust received too little punishment, then their children have had to shoulder a burden in their place. Hans Frank was hanged at Nuremberg, but his actions clearly affected his children deeply—particularly Niklas Frank. Only a very young boy when his father was Governor General, Niklas has written extensively of deep hatred towards his father.[3]

In other words, the crimes of the Nazis have left a sad personal heritage which has crossed the generations of victims and perpetrators alike. In legal, political and personal terms, therefore, the Holocaust continues to resonate. It has informed the way we frame our laws for decent society; it has remained a significant topic for debate in regard to how a number of political communities should understand themselves; and it continues to pose more personal challenges for families touched by the event. The

---

1 http://www.mail-archive.com/romania-news@yahoogroups.com/msg00806.html. (Consulted 27 February 2007.)
2 A. Hass, *The Aftermath: Living with the Holocaust* (CUP, 1996) and *In the Shadow of the Holocaust. The Second Generation* (CUP, 1996). See also M. Housden, 'The Mourning After. Memoir, Analysis and the Holocaust', in *European History Quarterly* 28 (1998) pp. 265–72.
3 N. Frank, *Der Vater: Eine Abrechnung* (Munich: Goldmann, 1993). See also G. Posner, *Hitler's Children: Inside the Families of the Third Reich* (London: Penguin, 1992).

history of the Holocaust certainly has provided us all with a warning about the extent of 'wrong' that Mankind can do when technology and bureaucracy are harnessed to hatred and ideological fervour. It is a highly-charged story which cannot be ignored and which should motivate us all to try to do better in the future. In this respect, study of the Holocaust shows how history is not 'just' about the past. It makes plain how 'the past' has helped frame the world we inhabit today and how it contributes to our identities. The Holocaust shows with particular clarity how the past can continue to live in the present.

Selected bibliography

The footnotes provide references for anyone who wants to follow up a theme in greater detail. It must be said, however, that the literature about the Holocaust is absolutely vast. Consequently the following brief bibliography is supposed to offer more concise assistance to readers still in the relatively early stages of finding out about the event. It identifies a few of the more interesting English-language sources on the Holocaust used in preparing this text.

Accessible introductory texts

Friedman, S. S. *A History of the Holocaust*. London: Valentine Mitchell, 2004.

Graml, H. *Antisemitism in the Third Reich*. Oxford: Blackwell, 1992.

Housden, M. *Resistance and Conformity in the Third Reich*. London: Routledge, 1997.

Marrus, M. R. *The Holocaust in History*. London: Penguin, 1993.

More advanced general texts

Aly, G. *Final Solution: Nazi Population Policy and the Murder of the European Jews*. London: Arnold, 1999.

Arad, Y., Gutman, I. and Margaliot, A. (eds.), *Documents on the Holocaust*. Jerusalem: Yad Vashem, 1996.

Bauer, Y. *Rethinking the Holocaust*. New Haven: Yale, 2002.

Hilberg, R. *The Destruction of the European Jews*. New York: New Viewpoints, 1973.

Mommsen, H. *From Weimar to Auschwitz*. Oxford: Polity Press, 1991.

Niewyk, D. L. (ed.) *The Holocaust: Problems and Perspectives of Interpretation*. Boston: Houghton Mifflin, 1997.

The event and those involved in it

Burleigh, M. and Wippermann, W. *The Racial State: Germany 1933 1945.* CUP, 1993.

Breitman, R. *The Architect of Genocide. Himmler and the Final Solution.* London: Bodley Head, 1991.

Browning, C. R. *The Path to Genocide. Essays in Launching the Final Solution.* CUP, 1992.

Gutman, Y. and Berenbaum, M. (eds.) *Anatomy of the Auschwitz Death Camp.* Bloomington: Indiana University Press, 1998.

Housden, M. *Hans Frank: Lebensraum and the Holocaust.* Basingstoke: Palgrave, 2003.

The background to anti-Semitism

Cohn, N. *Warrant for Genocide: The Myth of World-Conspiracy and the Protocols of the Elders of Zion.* Chico, CA: Scholars Press. 1981.

Lindemann, A. S. *Anti-Semitism before the Holocaust.* London: Longman, 2000.

Pulzer, P. *Jews and the German State.* Oxford: Blackwell, 1992.

Motivation and the perpetrators

Arendt, H. *Eichmann in Jerusalem: A Report on the Banality of Evil.* London: Penguin, 1994.

Baumann, Z. *Modernity and the Holocaust.* Oxford: Polity Press, 1989.

Browning, C. R. *Ordinary Men: Reserve Police Battalion 101 and the Final Solution in Poland.* New York: Harper Collins, 1993.

Finkelstein, N. G. and Birn, R. B. *A Nation on Trial: The Goldhagen Thesis and Historical Truth.* New York: Henry Holt, 1998.

Goldhagen, D. *Hitler's Willing Executioners: Ordinary Germans and the Holocaust.* London: Little, Brown and Company, 1996.

The reactions of bystanders

Bankier, D. *The Germans and the Final Solution*. Oxford: Blackwell, 1992.

Bankier, D. and Gutman, I. (eds.) *Nazi Europe and the Final Solution*. Jerusalem: Yad Vashem, 2003.

Dean, M. *Collaboration in the Holocaust: Crimes of the Local Police in Belorussia and Ukraine, 1941–44*. Basingstoke: Macmillan, 2000.

Gross, J. T. *Neighbours: The Destruction of the Jewish Community in Jedwabne, Poland, 1941*. London: Random House, 2003.

Rubinstein, W. D. *The Myth of Rescue*. London: Routledge, 1997.

Victims

Arad, Y. *Bełżec, Sobibór, Treblinka: The Operation Reinhard Death Camps*. Bloomington: Indiana University Press, 1987.

Grobman, A. and Landes, D. (eds.). *Critical Issues of the Holocaust*. Dallas, Texas: Rossell Books, 1983.

Roseman, M. *The Past in Hiding*. London: Penguin, 2000.

The legacy of the Holocaust

Evans, R. J. *In Hitler's Shadow: West German Historians and the Attempt to Escape from the Nazi Past*. London: I. B. Tauris, 1989.

Finkelstein, N. G. *The Holocaust Industry: Reflections on the Exploitation of Jewish Suffering*. London: Verso, 2000.

Hass, A. *The Aftermath: Living with the Holocaust*. CUP, 1996.

Robertson, G. *Crimes against Humanity: The Struggle for Global Justice*. London: Penguin, 2002.Humanities Insights

Also available from www.humanities-ebooks.co.uk

Humanities Insights

General Titles

An Inroduction to Feminist Theory
An Introduction to Critical Theory
An Introduction to Rhetorical Terms

Genre FictionSightlines

Octavia E Butler: *Xenogenesis / Lilith's Brood*
Reginal Hill: *On Beulah's Height*
Ian McDonald: *Chaga / Evolution's Store*
Walter Mosley: *Devil in a Blue Dress*
Tamora Pierce: *The Immortals*

History Insights

Oliver Cromwell
The British Empire: Pomp, Power and Postcolonialism
The Holocaust: Events, Motives, Legacy
Lenin's Revolution
Methodism and Society
The Risorgimento

Literature Insights

Conrad: *The Secret Agent*
Eliot, T S: 'The Love Song of J Alfred Prufrock' and *The Waste Land*
English Renaissance Drama: Theatre and Theatres in Shakespeare's Time
Faulkner: *The Sound and the Fury*
Gaskell, *Mary Barton*
Hardy: *Tess of the Durbervilles*
Ibsen: *The Doll's House*
Hopkins: Selected Poems
Ted Hughes: *New Selected Poems*
Lawrence: *Sons and Lovers*
Lawrence: *Women in Love*
Paul Scott: *The Raj Quartet*
Shakespeare: *Hamlet*
Shakespeare: *Henry IV*

Shakespeare: *Richard II*
Shakespeare: *Richard III*
Shakespeare: *The Tempest*
Shakespeare: *Troilus and Cressida*
Shelley: *Frankenstein*
Wordsworth: *Lyrical Ballads*
Fields of Agony: English Poetry and the First World War

Philosophy Insights

American Pragmatism
Contemporary Epistemology
Critical Thinking
Ethics
Existentialism
Formal Logic
Meta-Ethics
Contemporary Philosophy of Religion
Philosophy of Sport
Plato
Wittgenstein

Full Length Books

John Beer, *Blake's Humanism*
John Beer, *The Achievement of E M Forster*
John Beer, *Coleridge the Visionary*
Jared Curtis, ed.. *The Fenwick Notes of William Wordsworth*
Richard Gravil, *Master Narratives: Tellers and Telling in the English Novel*
Richard Gravil and Molly Lefebure, *The Coleridge Connection: Essays for Thomas McFarland*
Steven Duncan, *Analytic Philosophy of Religion: its History since 1955*
John K. Hale, *Milton as Multilingual: Selected Essays 1982–2004*
John Lennard, *Of Modern Dragons and other essays on Genre Fiction*
Colin Nicholson, *Fivefathers: Interviews with late Twentieth-Century Scottish Poets*
W J B Owen, *Understanding 'The Prelude'*
Keith Sagar, *D. H. Lawrence: Poet*
William Wordsworth, *The Prose Works of William Wordsworth*, Volume 1
William Wordsworth, *The Convention of Cintra*

www.ingramcontent.com/pod-product-compliance
Lightning Source LLC
Chambersburg PA
CBHW081500040426
42446CB00016B/3326